Only She Can Help Us!

Evil Forces Are Driving the World Toward War

*by **James Hanisch***

Introduction by **Father Nicholas Gruner**

Good Counsel Publications, Pound Ridge, New York

ISBN: 978-88-903559-5-0

To contact the publisher write or call:

Good Counsel Publications
P.O. Box 203
Pound Ridge, New York 10576-0203
United States of America
1-800-954-8737

To purchase extra copies retail or wholesale

In USA:
St. Joseph's Books
468 19th Street
Niagara Falls, New York 14301

In Canada:
Catholic Books
P.O. Box 693
Crystal Beach, Ontario
L0S 1R0

Call toll-free in North America 1-800-263-8160
1-905-871-7607 | Fax: 1-905-994-7054
www.fatima.org | E-mail: info@fatima.org

Photo Credits (see also photo credits on photo pages)
Part I, Chapter 1 Frontispiece — Photo by Hans Wendt. (Licensed under Fair use of copyrighted material via Wikipedia - http://en.wikipedia.org/wiki/File:WendtPSA.jpg#)

Part II, Chapter 1 Frontispiece — Photo courtesy of Andreas F. Borchert (licensed at http://commons.wikimedia.org/wiki/File:Clonmel_SS._Peter_and_Paul%27s_Church_West_Aisle_Window_08_Heart_of_Immaculate_Mary_2012_09_07.jpg#)

DEDICATION

"Peace on Earth to Men of Good Will"

This book is dedicated to the Immaculate Heart of the Blessed Virgin Mary, Whose promise of world peace gives us such great hope: "In the end My Immaculate Heart will triumph. The Holy Father will consecrate Russia to Me, Russia will be converted, and a period of peace will be given to mankind."

This book is also dedicated to all men of good will who are willing to defend, embrace, and promote the truth of Our Lady of Fatima's Message, and who are willing to think "outside of the box" provided by the mainstream media regarding the present geo-political situation.

This book is especially dedicated to those brave souls who are willing not only to face the truth of our situation, but also to work, to pray, and to sacrifice for the accomplishment of the peace predicted by Our Lady of Fatima for all mankind, by doing all they can to implement Her plan for peace — the only plan that will stop all wars, and the only plan that will stop the otherwise certain and obviously ever closer Fatima prophecy that "various nations will be annihilated'.

CONTENTS

INTRODUCTION

"I will put enmities between thee and the Woman, and thy seed and Her seed: She shall crush thy head, and thou shalt lie in wait for Her heel." (Gen. 3:15)

Dear Reader,

You hold a very important book in your hands.

Why is this book so important? We all need to step back and look at the situation in the world today in a larger context than the daily news can give us. We all need to realize that we are standing on the verge of what could be the final disaster for the vast majority of mankind.

We are falling into a MAJOR war — tragically, a war that is desired not only by the devil, but even by the powerful men who direct world affairs (to the extent that God allows), and who, like the devil, envision the enslavement of mankind under a New World Order.

It is no accident that the world's situation continues to worsen. Clearly, crises continue to arise and continue to escalate, by the purposeful actions of world powers.

Witness the recent (July 17, 2014) heartless destruction of the Malaysian Airlines flight (MH-17) crossing over Ukraine. Some nation or other's military was behind those terrible murders. Some nation or other's government wants to take the conflict between Russia and the West over Crimea and the ethnic Russians in eastern Ukraine to a higher level.

Recall also the fact (which *The Fatima Crusader* called attention to in Issue 109, page 45) that in the Maidan Square protests in Kiev (in February 2014), snipers on the building tops were shooting at both parties — police and protestors alike — purposely escalating the conflict.

The world is being intentionally driven to more and greater conflicts, more and greater wars.

It is not a matter of wild or baseless theorizing to say this — it is an officially recognized and acknowledged fact. In recent decades, world leaders have repeatedly made plans for war and used the media to stir up a popular appetite for war, and even deceived the public about a cause for war, knowing full well all the while that they had no grounds for war.

As the reader will see in Part I, Chapter 2 of this book, many damning facts of this kind have now come to light through the declassification of various official United States documents. This is the shocking picture that has emerged from the now-public facts regarding the 1962 Operation Northwoods and the Gulf of Tonkin Incident of August 1964 (which was used to precipitate direct U.S. involvement in the Vietnam War), as well as from the U.S. Congressional Record (in 2007 House Resolution 625), in which President Bush was censured for his false charges against Saddam Hussein (which led to the Iraq War).

The next major war, though, as you will read in this book, could well be more devastating for the whole world than anything the human race has ever experienced — and more terrible than any of us can imagine.

Since the time of this book's writing, events have continued to unfold in regard to the shooting down of Malaysia Airlines flight MH-17. Andrei Karaulov, a high-profile Russian journalist, in a recent feature on the Moscow Channel 5 "Moment of Truth" program has claimed to bring even more details to light about the perpetrators of this crime, including the name of the man who "pulled the trigger" on those 298 innocent lives. Four Ukrainian military jets with tail numbers 06, 07, 08 and 33 of the 229th squadron, Karaulov claims, intercepted the passenger plane. Lt. Col. Dmitro Jakazuz, piloting an SU-25 with tail number 08, shot the Boeing 777 down and has been in hiding in the United Arab Emirates since that day.

Without a truly proper and thorough investigation of the disaster and a transparent publication of the evidence — particularly all the black box data, all the Kiev control tower recordings on that day and all the U.S. satellite images of flight MH-17 — we will hear only the banter of accusations and counter-accusations. But in the meantime Russia is demonized and punished by the West as if it had been proven guilty of this terrible war crime.

Another Western trend, as described in this book, has been to steadily increase the militarization of NATO countries near Russia's borders, including the construction of anti-ballistic missile stations. While supposedly defensive in nature, these stations are in fact viewed by Russia as an intolerable threat. The same missiles housed in these stations which might be used as defensive interceptors can also be used in a first-strike offensive against Russia, delivering a virtually unstoppable close-range nuclear payload into the heart of Russia.

Things cannot continue to go on as they are, indefinitely. The world is on the edge of something momentous, whether for good or ill — either the promised Triumph of the Immaculate Heart of Mary, or the final descent into World War III. *We are very near to the end of our course, one way or the other.*

We need to use our voices to speak up, and to insist upon an impartial, thorough, complete investigation into the most recent *casus belli* (provocation for war) — the deliberate murder of 298 passengers and the destruction of Malaysian Airlines flight MH-17. The public must be allowed to know all the facts.

I thank my friend James Hanisch for drawing the facts together for us in a way that allows us to see plainly what the distortions and omissions of the mainstream media have obscured.

We must act now, and quickly, to honor Our Lady of Fatima's requests (see Part II). Obedience to the Message of Fatima is our only hope and our only solution. Above all, what is needed is the Pope's and the Catholic bishops' obedience to God's command to consecrate Russia to the Immaculate Heart of Mary in the solemn and public manner specified by Our Lady of Fatima. Our time is running out.

Our Lord expects us to do our part in acting for Our Lady's honor and for our own preservation by using the moral influence of whatever station each of us has in life, as well as our prayers, to bring about the Pope's obedience.

We must also pray our Holy Rosary every day, asking for Our Lady's protection on our families, on our neighborhoods and parishes, on our friends and co-workers, on our cities and our whole nations. We must insist that the Pope and the bishops of the Catholic Church obey Our Lady of Fatima before it is too late for all of us.

Father Nicholas Gruner

Father Nicholas Gruner, B.Com., S.T.L., S.T.D. (Cand.)
The Fatima Center, December 8, 2014
The Feast of the Immaculate Conception

Part I:
The Imminent Danger of World War III

The victims murdered aboard Malaysia Airlines Flight 17 (MH-17) in eastern Ukraine on July 17, 2014 may have endured a terrifying plummet to the ground similar to that experienced by those aboard Pacific Southwest Airlines Flight 182 in September 1978 (pictured above). The great difference between the two disasters was that MH-17's demise was no accident. It was deliberately shot down. On whose soil will the next war-triggering event be carried out?

CHAPTER I • *The First Act of World War III?* *The Murder of 298 People*

BUK-M1 missiles are capable of hitting flying targets at an altitude of 22 km (72,000 ft) — more than twice the height at which the downed Malaysian plane was flying.

On July 17, 2014, a civilian passenger plane was shot down as it neared the Russian border of Ukraine. Two hundred and ninety-eight people were murdered by this act.

Was the attack on Malaysia Airlines Flight MH-17 intended to escalate the conflict in Ukraine into a war between NATO powers and Russia? Some believe that President Obama, Secretary of State John Kerry, and British Prime Minister David Cameron are determined to use the incident for this end.

On the day following the incident, President Obama made a speech indicting the "Russian-backed" separatists in Ukraine for the attack, stressing repeatedly President Putin's blame in the affair for supporting the separatists.[1] John Kerry followed suit, insisting: "Russia is supporting these separatists. Russia is arming these separatists. Russia is training these separatists…";[2] and Prime Minister Cameron called the disaster "an outrage made in Moscow."[3]

---

[1] Cf. "Transcript: President Obama's July 18 statement on Ukraine and Gaza," *The Washington Post*, http://www.washingtonpost.com/politics/transcript-obamas-statement-on-ukraine-and-gaza/2014/07/18/a3224560-0e8c-11e4-8c9a-923ecc0c7d23_story.html

[2] "Rebels Were Given Anti-Aircraft Missile Training In RUSSIA, Claims Kerry As Pentagon Intelligence Reveals 150 Tanks, Missile Launchers and Armoured Vehicles Crossed into Ukraine Days Before Disaster," Associated Press and *Daily Mail Reporter*, July 20, 2014; http://www.dailymail.co.uk/news/article-2699235/US-outlines-case-against-Russia-downed-plane.html

[3] "David Cameron: This Is an Outrage Made in Moscow…" July 20, 2014, *The Sunday Times*; http://www.thesundaytimes.co.uk/sto/news/world_news/Ukraine/article1436658.ece

But while these high-level Western spokesmen were quick to allege that the pro-Russian separatists in Ukraine had shot down the plane with a BUK surface-to-air missile supplied by Russia, they made little effort to provide credible evidence for their claim. William Engdahl of *Veterans Today* reports:

"Most of the Obama Administration arguments about who was responsible for downing the MH17 derive from statements made by Kiev government officials. ... Just hours after the news of the downing of the plane, Ukrainian Secret Intelligence released what it claimed was 'proof' that the MH17 was shot down by Russian-trained separatists, 'militants of the Bes group' using a Russian anti-aircraft missile under direct orders from Russia. ...

"All this Kiev 'smoking gun' evidence presented on YouTube swiftly vanished when diligent IT researchers discovered that the time/date stamp showed that the video was put online on 2014-07-16 at 19:10 [7:10 pm] Kiev time — a full day BEFORE the downing of MH17. ...

"In a July 21 Washington press briefing, State Department Assistant Secretary Victoria Nuland's press spokesperson, Marie Harf, was asked why, if Secretary John Kerry and the US Government possessed 'irrefutable' evidence of Russian and rebel involvement in MH17, were they refusing to make it public...? Harf merely referred to July 20 statements by Kerry, saying that 'our assessment is that this was an SA-11 fired from Russian-backed, separatist-controlled territory.'

"When pressed again for proof, she said that 'we saw it in social media afterwards, we saw videos, we saw photos of the pro-Russian separatists bragging about shooting down an aircraft...' She did not explain how she had seen a talking photograph, however.

"A day later, on July 22, CNN (a loyal mouthpiece of the State Department) announced that the US Government had now published satellite evidence. It was [a] drawing[4]..., which any photo-paint novice could have made, showing nothing which could be proven in any independent evidential inquiry.

"When this too failed to persuade doubters, the Obama Administration went into frantic 'damage control' mode. At 5:57 pm Washington time on July 22, they decided to organize an anonymous press briefing... [at which they] admitted that 'the US had no direct evidence that the missile used to

---

[4] See the graphic in Tyler Durden, "US Government Releases Alleged Evidence Of MH17 Missile Trajectory," July 22, 2014; http://www.zerohedge.com/news/2014-07-22/us-government-releases-alleged-evidence-mh17-missile-trajectory

2

shoot down the passenger jet came from Russia.' They then added that they didn't know whether any Russian operatives were present at the missile launch and were 'not certain' that the missile crew had been trained in Russia. In terms of who fired the missile, they stated, 'We don't know a name, we don't know a rank and we're not even 100 percent sure of a nationality…'"[5]

Others, on the contrary, believe that the separatists had nothing to do with the incident — and further, that the separatists have neither a BUK missile system nor any personnel trained in its use.

The Ukrainian militia, however, is known to have BUK missiles.

Very significant, too, is the fact that for some unknown reason, the MH-17 deviated its course from the international aviation corridor by 14 km as it neared Donetsk, taking it directly over the area of conflict between Ukrainian and separatist forces.

Russia Responds

Russia responded to the accusations of its involvement in the attack with a press conference on July 21, at which the Russian Defense Ministry released its pertinent military intelligence data. Speaking in Moscow, Lt. Gen. Andrei Kartapolov (head of the Russian General Staff's Main Operations Directorate) began by raising the pointed question of why the plane had been flying through that combat zone — was it due to a navigational error, or was the pilot *directed to that course by Ukrainian air traffic control?* We will have the answer to these critical questions, he said, when the real evidence in this matter is forthcoming from the black-box recordings and the air traffic control communications.

Kartapolov also displayed a series of satellite photos of Ukrainian BUK anti-aircraft missile batteries, demonstrating that official Ukrainian forces had moved a BUK launcher to the Donetsk region on the day of the crash. What was the purpose, Kartapolov asked, of deploying such a large group of air defense systems near Donetsk?

> "On the day that the Malaysian airliner crashed, the Ukrainian forces deployed an air defense group of three or four BUK-M1 missile batteries near Donetsk. … For what purpose and against whom were these missile systems deployed? As is known, the [separatists'] militia has no aviation."[6]

Further, these missile systems were confirmed to have been active on the day of the disaster, as radiation from the component Kupol radar was detected by the

---

[5]   F. William Engdahl, "NEO – Another Journalist Exposes MH17 False Flag," *Veterans Today: Military and Foreign Affairs Journal*, August 21, 2014; http://www.veteranstoday.com/2014/08/21/neo-another-journalist-exposes-mh17-false-flag/

[6]   Cited in Tyler Durden, "Russia Says Has Photos Of Ukraine Deploying BUK Missiles In East, Radar Proof Of Warplanes In MH17 Vicinity," July 21, 2014, *Zero Hedge*; http://www.zerohedge.com/news/2014-07-21/russia-says-has-photos-ukraine-deploying-buk-missiles-east-rader-proof-warplanes-mh1 Watch the press conference with English dubbing on RT at http://rt.com/news/174412-malaysia-plane-russia-ukraine/

Russian military, emanating from Styla (a village lying 30 km south of Donetsk).[7]

Machine Gun Bullet Holes

But was it actually a surface-to-air missile that brought the plane down? Kartapolov stated that Russian radar detected another plane in the area —a Ukrainian SU-25 military jet, whose presence was confirmed on video taken by the Russian regional air traffic control center in Rostov. This second plane made a rapid ascent toward the Malaysian aircraft, approaching within a distance of only 3-5 km from it just at the time when it was shot down. The jet then circled above the crash site for about 4 minutes.

"[We] would like to get an explanation as to why the military jet was flying along a civil aviation corridor at almost the same time and at the same level as a passenger plane," Kartapolov remarked.

The presence of the Ukrainian fighter jet (or jets?) was confirmed in a BBC report, citing multiple eye-witnesses who specifically indicated that a military aircraft was flying alongside the Malaysian Flight MH-17 at the time that it was shot down. Correspondent Olga Ivshina writes:

The BUK M1 target acquisition radar is capable of detecting and recognizing flying targets at a range of up to 160 km. Besides providing guidance data for BUK missiles, the radar system is also commonly used to assist fighter jets, alone or in groups, in their Air Superiority and ambush operations. Russian intelligence sources detected radiation from an active BUK system radar near Donetsk on the day of the Malaysian flight's destruction.

"The inhabitants of the nearby villages are certain that they saw military aircraft in the sky shortly prior to the catastrophe. According to them, it actually was the jet fighters that brought down the Boeing.

"Eyewitness #1: There were two explosions in the air. And this is how it broke apart. And [the fragments] blew apart like this, to the sides. And when …

"Eyewitness #2: … And there was another aircraft, a military one,

---

[7] Pete Papaherakles, "Who Really Shot Down Malaysian Flight MH17?" *American Free Press*, Issue 34, p. 14, August 25, 2014; http://americanfreepress.net/?p=19132

4

beside it. Everybody saw it.

"Eyewitness #1: Yes, yes. It was flying under it, because it could be seen. It was proceeding underneath, below the civilian one.

"Eyewitness #3: There were sounds of an explosion. But they were in the sky. They came from the sky. Then this plane made a sharp turn-around like this. It changed its trajectory and headed in that direction [indicating the direction with her hands]."[8]

A report issued by the Russian Union of Engineers echoed Kartapolov's doubts about the claim that it was a BUK missile which brought the plane down. When these missiles are launched, the Union of Engineers pointed out, everyone within a 7-10 km radius knows about it. Both the launch and the flight of the missile are accompanied by loud noises, and the missile's flight is easily observed by its persistent, billowing exhaust trail. These signs are impossible to conceal, yet no one in that well-populated region reported seeing or hearing any such things. The Engineers' report states:

"The narrative detailing the use of the BUK M1 Rocket complex [in the attack on MH-17], in the opinion of our experts, contains a number of issues which render it open to doubt as an accurate chronicle of events. …. [T]he launch of a BUK M1 missile is accompanied by the following significant audio-visual effects: There is a powerful explosion at the launch site, … [producing] a great deal of noise both at launch and during the missile flight. … There is a trail of exhaust created by the missile as a result of the burning of fuel during its flight. … The launch trails extend to the clouds and will remain in the air for up to 10 minutes. The sound of the rocket launch is audible to anyone standing within a radius of 7-10 km from the launch site, …[and the white launch trail would] be visible to those standing in a radius of within 10 km from the missile launch site. …

"The airliner was shot down in daylight, in a highly populated area, in the presence not only of military participants following the situation in the skies, but also journalists who were armed with cameras, as well as those people who inhabited the area who were correspondingly equipped with telephones and cameras. Here, it should also be remarked, that, not one person, but at least a military squad would be present at the launch of a BUK M1 missile and that this would make its concealment impossible."[9]

---

[8]   Olga Ivshina, "The Catastrophe of MH17: BBC in the Search of the 'BUK,'" July 23, 2014, BBC Russian Service, relayed by *Global Research News*, July 27, 2014, "Deleted BBC Report. 'Ukrainian Fighter Jet Shot Down MHI7,' Donetsk Eyewitnesses"; http://www.globalresearch.ca/deleted-bbc-report-ukrainian-fighter-jet-shot-down-mhi7-donetsk-eyewitnesses/5393631

[9]   Informational Briefing by Ivan A. Andrievskii, Vice President of Russian Union of Engineers, "Analysis of the causes of the crash of Flight MH17 (Malaysian Boeing 777)," pp. 6-8, August 15, 2014; English translation at http://www.globalresearch.ca/wp-content/uploads/2014/09/MH17_Report_Russian_Union_

The launch of a BUK M1 missile is like a city on a hill — it cannot be hidden. The launch explosion is so loud that it is heard as far away as 10 km. If there had actually been a BUK ground-to-air missile shot at MH-17, a great many of the locals would have witnessed and testified to the launch, and posted pictures of the condensation trail (visible for 10 minutes) on social media sites.

What might have been the cause of those noises "in the air" described by the eye-witnesses? The Russian Engineers' report continues:

"The nature of the holes on the fragments of the skin surfaces and fuselage ... allows us to assert that it was missiles/gunfire from an aircraft that was used. ... This is indicated by the pattern of damage and the dispersal of the fragments: there are round holes, which are typically produced as a result of gun shots, and discontinuous holes characteristic of flechette rockets. ... [I]t is evident from the way the holes are arranged in the fragments of the flat surfaces and the fuselage that they do not reflect the typical picture of the impact of 'BUK M1' missiles, which would have left a very noticeable and characteristic pattern of damage marks. In this case, it is clear that there are no such traces on the debris fragments. ...

"[T]he entry and exit holes in the cockpit of the Boeing 777 are fully consistent with the passage through the plane of shells from the 20-30 mm caliber guns found on military aircraft. ... Sighting was targeted in the area of the cockpit; while the shells that broke through the cockpit proceeded out the other side. ... On the trim panel the characteristic entry holes are visible as well as some exit points. The edges of the entry holes are bent inward; they are much smaller and are circular in shape. The exit openings are less clearly formed; their edges are torn outward. ... Thus, according to the analysts from the Russian Union of Engineers, we have the complete destruction of the Boeing 777 as a result of missile systems using 'air to air' close combat missiles as well as a 30 mm aircraft cannon. ..."

of_Engineers140818.pdf See the original Russian text at http://www.globalresearch.ca/wp-content/uploads/2014/09/MH17_Report_Russian_Union_of_Engineers_RU_Original.pdf

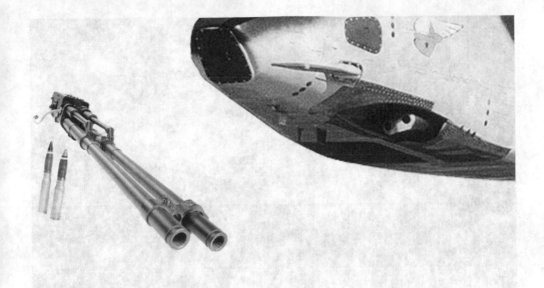

An SU-25 fighter jet is equipped with dual-barrel 30mm cannons, which can be used in aerial combat to inflict damage of precisely the type evidenced in the Malaysian Flight MH-17 wreckage. The bullets typically pass through an aircraft in a concentrated configuration, producing neatly rounded perforations with the edges of entry holes pushed inward and the edges of holes on the opposite wall pushed outward.

U.S. Satellite Evidence — Where Is It?!

Kartapolov also pointed out that there was an American spy satellite above the area where the Malaysian plane was attacked at the time of its destruction. He urged the U.S. to settle the matter by making the satellite's photos and data available to international expert investigators. Kartapolov concluded:

"I would like to say that the information we have presented here is based on objective and reliable data from various technical systems. The same cannot be said of the unsubstantiated accusations that have been made against Russia."[10]

President Putin's comments stressed that the local task force investigating the crash site was inadequate to the scale of the incident. Calling for an independent expert investigation headed by the International Civil Aviation Organization (ICAO), he cautioned the West: "In the meantime, no one has the right to use this tragedy to achieve their narrowly selfish political goals."[11]

---

[10] Lt. Gen. Kartapolov went on to cite an example: "Media outlets have circulated a video supposedly showing a BUK system being transported from Ukraine to Russia. This is clearly a fabrication. This video was made in the town of Krasnoarmeysk, as evidenced by the billboard you see in the background, advertising a car dealership at 34 Dnepropetrovsk Street. Krasnoarmeysk has been controlled by the Ukrainian military since May 11." (See the video he speaks of in the July 21, 2014 RT report, "10 More Questions Russian Military Pose to Ukraine, US over MH17 Crash," at http://rt.com/news/174496-malaysia-crash-russia-questions/)

[11] "Putin: Taskforce at Malaysia MH17 Crash Site Not Enough, Full-Scale Intl. Team Needed," *RT*, July 20, 2014; http://rt.com/news/174268-ukraine-mh17-crash-putin/

It appears from the damage inflicted on the cockpit panels that a military fighter jet fired directly on the pilot of the Malaysia Airlines plane with a 0.30 caliber machine gun. Reporter Alex Lantier of *OpEdNews* calls this discovery "a powerful accusation not only against the Ukrainian government, but against Washington, Berlin, and their European allies. ... These forces now stand accused not only of stoking an explosive political and military confrontation with Russia on its border with Ukraine over the MH17 crash, which threatens to erupt into nuclear war, but of provoking the confrontation through the cold-blooded murder of 298 people aboard MH17." (Photo credit: BULENT KILIC/AFP/Getty Images)

Malaysia's Verdict

Malaysian intelligence sources seem to concur with Russia in suggesting that Ukraine was the culprit. Alex Lantier of *OpEdNews* reports:

"A Thursday article in the *New Straits Times*, Malaysia's flagship English-language newspaper, charged the US- and European-backed Ukrainian regime in Kiev with shooting down Malaysian Airlines flight MH17 in east Ukraine last month. Given the tightly controlled character of the Malaysian media, it appears that the accusation that Kiev shot down MH17 has the imprimatur of the Malaysian state. ...

"[The article] lays out evidence that Ukrainian fighter aircraft attacked the jetliner with first a missile, then with bursts of 30-millimeter machine gun fire from both sides of MH17. The Russian army has already presented detailed radar and satellite data showing a Ukrainian Sukhoi-25 fighter jet tailing MH17 shortly before the jetliner crashed. ... It cited 'experts who had said that the photographs of the blast fragmentation patterns on the fuselage of the airliner showed two distinct shapes — the shredding pattern associated with a warhead packed with "flechettes," and the more uniform, round-type penetration holes consistent with that of cannon rounds....' [Also pictured was] photographic evidence of MH17 wreckage suggesting that cockpit panels were raked [*i.e.*, shot with a dense spray of bullets] with heavy machine gun fire from both the port and starboard sides."[12]

Irresponsible Withholding of Major Evidence

The cockpit voice recorder and the flight data recorder were recovered intact by the separatists in Donetsk, who (apparently sensing nothing to fear from the truth) immediately handed them over to Malaysian authorities. Malaysia acknowledged that the "black boxes" had not been tampered with, and passed them on to the Dutch Safety Board (DSB), which was given the task of investigating the incident since the majority of passengers on the flight were from the Netherlands.

The DSB stated in its report that the cockpit of the plane had been penetrated by "a large number of high-energy objects that penetrated the aircraft from the outside."[13]

---

12   Alex Lantier, *OpEdNews*, " Malaysian Press Charges Ukraine Government Shot Down MH 17," August 9, 2014; http://www.opednews.com/articles/Malaysian-press-charges-Uk-by-Alex-Lantier-Government-Corruption_Malaysia-Airlines-Flight-17_Putin_Russia-140809-576.html See also articles by Eric Zuesse at http://www.infowars.com/ukrainian-government-su-25-fighter-jets-shot-down-malaysian-airliner/ http://www.globalresearch.ca/german-pilot-speaks-out-shocking-analysis-of-the-shooting-down-of-malaysian-mh17/5394111 and http://www.globalresearch.ca/evidence-is-now-conclusive-two-ukrainian-government-fighter-jets-shot-down-malaysian-airlines-mh17-it-was-not-a-buk-surface-to-air-missile/5394814

13   "Preliminary Report: Crash Involving Malaysia Airlines Boeing 777-200 Flight MH17, Hrabove, Ukraine–17 July 2014," p. 25; http://www.anderweltonline.com/fileadmin/user_upload/PDF/b3923acad0ceprem-rapport-mh-17-en-interactief.pdf See also Christof Lehmann, "DSB Report: Malaysia Airlines MH17 Probably Shot Down – Cover-up Continues," September 9, 2014, *NSNBC International*; http://nsnbc.me/2014/09/09/dsb-report-malaysia-airlines-mh17-probably-shot-down-coverup-continues/

Going only so far as to say that the objects originated from outside the fuselage, the report is silent as to what these objects were likely to have been, whether shrapnel from a missile or bullets from a machine gun. The report also presents a suspicious, virtually blank "transcript" of the final 14 minutes of the cockpit voice recording. Peter Haisenko, a 30-year veteran pilot for Europe's largest airline, Lufthansa, comments on the report:

"One thing must be stated outright: This report does not lie. It just can't lie since there is nothing new in it. I myself have never seen such a meaningless plane crash report. What comes as a surprise, however, is the report's diplomatic, sophisticated choice of words, which loses itself in ambiguous terminology. It was probably planned this way, so each party can continue to defend their version of what happened with zeal. …

"The term 'high-energy objects' is totally original. What is this? I myself know this term from astrophysics or quantum physics. Otherwise, I have not commonly seen it in the context of aviation or plane accidents. So how should this concept be understood? …

"This strange wording leaves everything open. Those who want to follow the Western description can conclude that a surface-to-air missile discharges 'high-energy-objects.' This is precisely the interpretation that I observed in the German media today.

"Our newspapers are reciting like a creed the American version of the cause of the disaster, issued immediately after the MH 017 crash, by claiming that the present report confirms that the Boeing 777 was shot down by a surface-to-air missile.

"That is not exactly what the report states, but it allows this interpretation — and that's probably the point of this very flexible choice of words. Everybody can interpret what they want to believe according to their own taste. …

"The transcript of the radio communication starts at 13:08:00 and ends at 13:22:02, a 14 minute time frame. From my experience as an aircraft captain I cannot imagine that during 14 minutes no other dialogues or sounds were picked up in the cockpit by the voice recorder. When the cockpit receives radio transmissions from other aircraft, those are also recorded by the device.

"As I said, there are no lies, but in all likelihood, not everything is being said. …

"This 'report' is not worth the paper it is written on. This is not surprising, because the Kiev Maidan government had to give their OK to what could be published."[14]

In addition to the obfuscations of the Dutch Safety Board (DSB) report, there were a number of even more telling departures from normal investigative procedures which took place in the case of MH-17. Peter Haisenko also writes:

When an airplane crashes, within 24 hours there are usually legions of experts at the scene who register everything in detail and start collecting the debris. First of all experts of the plane manufacturer are sent to the scene — in this case Boeing — followed by the NTSB (National Transportation Safety Board), and by specialists and experts from the countries concerned. In addition to the flight recorder, these specialists are responsible for an examination of the debris. Normally, the airplane is reconstructed from the pieces in order to determine the cause of the crash.

Yet in the case of MH 017 normal procedures were not followed. No representatives from Boeing appeared on the site. The airliner was not pieced together in order to determine the cause of its destruction. The information in the black boxes has not been revealed. Therefore, we have to arrive at a conclusion based on experience and the information available. ...

The West has control of the investigation and apparently has decided not to investigate. However, we do have two critical pieces of information. One is the report of the Canadian representative of the Organization for Security and Co-operation in Europe (OSCE) that reports bullet holes in the cockpit section of the airliner. Photos are available that clearly show bullet holes in the pattern of machine gun fire on both sides of the airliner's cockpit. The other piece of information comes from a report in the Malaysian newspaper *New Straits Times* that intelligence analysts have concluded that one of the airliner's engines was hit by a **heat-seeking air-to-air missile**. We know[15] that there were Ukrainian jets armed with such weapons close to the airliner at the time that it crashed.

These two pieces of information support my conclusion of what happened based on my experience and my research:

A warplane fired an air-to-air missile which hit the right engine of MH 017. In the cockpit of the MH 017 only a violent shock could be perceived,

---

[14]   Peter Haisenko, "Camouflage and Cover-Up: The Dutch Commission Report on the Malaysian MH17 Crash is 'Not Worth the Paper it's Written On,'" September 11, 2014, *Global Research*; http://www.globalresearch.ca/camouflage-and-coverup-the-dutch-commission-report-on-the-malaysian-mh17-crash-is-not-worth-the-paper-its-written-on/5400990

[15]   Mr. Haisenko cites here Haris Hussain, "US Analysts Conclude MH17 Downed by Aircraft," *New Straits Times Online*, August 7, 2014; http://www.nst.com.my/node/20925

along with the fire alarm and the failure notice of engine number two. Pilots would be aware of engine failure, not of a missile strike.

The missile hit might have caused a strong yawning moment and an immediate drop in speed. The pilots instantly had to initiate emergency procedures for this emergency, and were concentrated on it with full attention.

According to procedural rule, the pilots had to turn the engine off, isolate it, reduce speed and altitude. Afterwards they had to select and head for an emergency landing place and inform the ground control about their emergency situation as soon as possible. A captain in an emergency situation may do everything to save his plane, his own life and the lives of his passengers.

He has the so-called "emergency authority" that allows actions outside of any provision. The nearest major airport for the pilots of MH 017 for an emergency landing was probably Kiev. Rostov in Russia was closer, but in order to go to Rostov the pilots would have had to cope with a change of the control center and a border crossing, which would have meant extra stress.

MH 017 had therefore initiated a curve back towards Kiev in connection with a descent. Now just imagine, that MH 017 would have landed in Kiev. In Kiev it could not have been disguised that the airliner had been hit by an air-to-air missile. The emergency landing procedure had to be prevented – no matter on what airport. This was achieved by machine gun fire.[16]

Images from the U.S. spy satellite which was directly above the doomed plane when it was attacked could settle the questions surrounding this terrible incident in which 298 people lost their lives, but U.S. authorities have refused to release those pictures, or even to utter a word acknowledging the satellite's presence in the area. Neither have the air traffic control recordings been released, after being immediately seized by Ukrainian authorities.[17] William Engdahl sums up the situation:

"The burning question is why the US Government has not released the exact tracking images for flight MH-17, which show precisely where it flew and from precisely where it was hit? Could it be they are afraid to reveal what they have because it shows exactly the opposite of what they

---

[16]   Peter Haisenko, "The Evidence: MH 017," September 4, 2014, emphasis added; Guest Column posted at http://www.paulcraigroberts.org/2014/09/04/25636/

[17]   *Cf.* Tyler Durden, "Ukraine's Security Service Has Confiscated Air Traffic Control Recordings With Malaysian Jet," *Zero Hedge*, July 19, 2014, http://www.zerohedge.com/news/2014-07-18/ukraines-security-service-has-confiscated-air-traffic-control-recordings-malaysian-j and Haris Hussain and Tasnim Lokman, "Malaysia Wants the 'Missing' Ukrainian ATC Tapes," *New Straits Times*, August 8, 2014, http://www.nst.com.my/node/21260

are saying it does?"

This is also the view of a member of the Russian Federal Security Services interviewed by journalist Richard Walker:

"The one thing we can be certain of is, they have evidence, but the question is, what does it show? … If the CIA and NSA had evidence from their satellites that militias or the Russian military shot MH17 out of the sky, they would have produced it for the world, … [but] if it shows the plane was taken down by an R-60 missile fired by the SU-25 or by a Buk-launched missile, or both, are they going to tell the world that their allies in Kiev were responsible?[18]

Walker adds his own assessment of the Western media's failure to consider or report on the important facts of the matter:

"Within 24 hours of the downing of Malaysian Airlines Flight MH17 over eastern Ukraine, Washington and the mass media pointed an accusing finger at Russia without a shred of evidence. …

"Russia's military has produced satellite images showing that the Ukrainian military had a BUK battery in eastern Ukraine close the city of Lugansk on July 14, three days before the plane was downed. More telling is Kartapolov's satellite evidence showing that the same missile battery was moved close to the area controlled by the militias shortly before the plane was shot out of the sky, and that there were at least nine Ukrainian military radars, used to control the BUK, functioning on July 17, the fateful day.

"For Kartapolov, an even stranger fact is those radars went silent the next day. No reason has been offered by Kiev or its backers for the highly unusual radar activity at such a critical juncture. …

"The [Ukrainian SU-25] fighter would have been visible to the satellites with which the National Security Agency (NSA) and the Central Intelligence Agency (CIA) had been watching eastern Ukraine for months. Neither intelligence agency has commented on the Russian claim. Meanwhile, Washington's ally, the Kiev government, has refused to acknowledge or explain why one of its jets was so close to the doomed plane. …

"That uncomfortable truth has been ignored and denied … by the Western media in the rush to judgment to blame Russia…. [More recently,] the initial efforts to portray Russia as the bad guy to further damage the image of Russian President Vladimir Putin and provide a case for added

---

18   Richard Walker, "Available Evidence Shows Ukrainian Missile Battery Shot Down Malaysian Plane," *American Free Press*, September 3, 2014; http://americanfreepress.net/?p=19317

economic sanctions against Russia have been replaced by a deafening silence and a willingness to deny the public evidence, which could point to the real perpetrators."[19]

Award-winning American investigative journalist Robert Parry (best known for his coverage of the Iran-Contra affair for the *Associated Press* and *Newsweek*) recently castigated the Western mainstream media for its reckless and unprofessional journalism. Parry warns that by parroting unverified claims from biased sources, U.S. news outlets risk propelling the world into a nuclear confrontation.

The most far-reaching voice challenging the mainstream Western media has been that of investigative journalist Robert Parry, who fears that our Western leaders and media alike are rolling the dice in a deadly game, with all of our lives on the line. Washington and the U.S. media's refusal to acknowledge an important body of evidence in their rush to blame Russia, he believes, has engendered a widespread ignorance and prejudice that could lead the United States into a war with Russia:

"In the heat of the U.S. media's latest war hysteria — rushing to pin blame for the crash of a Malaysia Airlines passenger jet on Russia's President Vladimir Putin — there is the same absence of professional skepticism that has marked similar stampedes on Iraq, Syria and elsewhere — with key questions not being asked or answered.

"The dog-not-barking question on the catastrophe over Ukraine is: what did the U.S. surveillance satellite imagery show? It's hard to believe that — with the attention that U.S. intelligence has concentrated on eastern Ukraine for the past half year that the alleged trucking of several large BUK anti-aircraft missile systems from Russia to Ukraine and then back to Russia didn't show up somewhere.

"Yes, there are limitations to what U.S. spy satellites can see. But the BUK missiles are about 16 feet long and they are usually mounted on trucks or tanks. Malaysia Airlines Flight 17 also went down during the afternoon, not at night, meaning the missile battery was not concealed by darkness.

"So why hasn't this question of U.S. spy-in-the-sky photos — and what

---

[19]   *Ibid.*

14

they reveal — been pressed by the major U.S. news media? How can the *Washington Post* run front-page stories, such as the one on Sunday with the definitive title 'U.S. Official: Russia Gave Systems,' without demanding from these U.S. officials details about what the U.S. satellite images disclose?

"Instead, the *Post*'s Michael Birnbaum and Karen DeYoung wrote from Kiev: 'The United States has confirmed that Russia supplied sophisticated missile launchers to separatists in eastern Ukraine and that attempts were made to move them back across the Russian border after the Thursday shoot-down of a Malaysian jetliner, a U.S. official said Saturday.' …

"Instead of pressing for … details, the U.S. mainstream press has simply passed on the propaganda coming from the Ukrainian government and the U.S. State Department.…

"Much of the rest of the known case against Russia comes from claims made by the Ukrainian regime, which emerged from the unconstitutional *coup d'etat* against elected President Viktor Yanukovych on Feb. 22. … [But] the Kiev regime actually has a terrible record of telling the truth or pursuing serious investigations of human rights crimes.

"Still left open are questions about the identity of snipers who on Feb. 20 fired on both police and protesters at the Maidan, touching off the violent escalation that led to Yanukovych's ouster. Also, the Kiev regime has failed to ascertain the facts about the death-by-fire of scores of ethnic Russians in the Trade Union Building in Odessa on May 2.[20]

"The Kiev regime also duped the *New York Times* (and apparently the U.S. State Department) when it disseminated photos that supposedly showed Russian military personnel inside Russia and then later inside Ukraine. After the State Department endorsed the 'evidence,' the *Times* led its newspaper with this story on April 21, but it turned out that one of the key photos supposedly shot in Russia was actually taken in Ukraine, destroying the premise of the story.[21]

"But here we are yet again with the MSM [*i.e.*, mainstream media] relying on unverified claims being made by the Kiev regime about something as sensitive as whether Russia provided sophisticated anti-aircraft missiles — capable of shooting down high-flying civilian aircraft — to poorly trained eastern Ukrainian rebels.

---

[20]   For more about this topic, see Robert Parry, "Burning Ukraine's Protesters Alive," Consortiumnews.com, May 10, 2014; http://consortiumnews.com/2014/05/10/burning-ukraines-protesters-alive/

[21]   For more about this topic, see Robert Parry, "*NYT* Retracts Russian-Photo Scoop," Consortiumnews.com, April 23, 2014; http://consortiumnews.com/2014/04/23/nyt-retracts-russian-photo-scoop/

"This charge is so serious that it could propel the world into a second Cold War and conceivably — if there are more such miscalculations — into a nuclear confrontation.

"These moments call for the utmost in journalistic professionalism, especially skepticism toward propaganda from biased parties. Yet what Americans have seen again is the major U.S. news outlets, led by the *Washington Post* and the *New York Times*, publishing the most inflammatory of articles based largely on unreliable Ukrainian officials and on the U.S. State Department which was a principal instigator of the Ukraine crisis.

"In the recent past, this sort of sloppy American journalism has led to mass slaughters in Iraq — and has contributed to near U.S. wars on Syria and Iran — but now the stakes are much higher.

"As much fun as it is to heap contempt on a variety of 'designated villains,' such as Saddam Hussein, Bashar al-Assad, Ali Khamenei, and now Vladimir Putin, this sort of recklessness is careening the world toward a very dangerous moment, conceivably its last."[22]

"The End of the Story"

Western media sources have essentially laid the incident's story to rest, accepting Washington's claims without insisting that the real and conclusive evidence in the matter ever be produced. Dr. Paul Craig Roberts, however, (former Assistant Secretary of the Treasury under President Reagan and former associate editor of the *Wall Street Journal*) is one who is little inclined to accept Washington's story simply on good faith. He is perhaps excessively plain-spoken, but he offers important advice:

"Keep in mind that a totally corrupt White House, over the objections of its own intelligence agencies, sent the Secretary of State to the United Nations to lie to the world about Iraqi weapons of mass destruction that the White House knew did not exist. The consequences are that millions were killed, maimed, and displaced....

"The Obama regime lied on the basis of concocted 'evidence' that Assad had used chemical weapons against the Syrian people, thus crossing the 'red line' that the White House had drawn, justifying a US military attack on the Syrian people.[23] The Russian government exposed the fake evidence,

---

22   Robert Parry, "What Did US Spy Satellites See in Ukraine?" Consortiumnew.com, July 20, 2014; http://consortiumnews.com/2014/07/20/what-did-us-spy-satellites-see-in-ukraine/

23   In another place, Roberts adds: "When Washington drew a 'red line' in the sand with regard to the Syrian government's use of chemical weapons against the outside forces that Washington had organized and sent into Syria to overthrow the government, all the while pretending that these Islamists mercenaries were the true spokesmen for democracy in Syria, most of the world knew that Washington was about to organize a

and the British Parliament voted down any UK participation in the Obama regime's attack on Syria. Left isolated, the Obama regime dared not assume the obvious role of war criminal. …

"Keep in mind that both the George W. Bush and Obama regimes have also lied through their teeth about 'Iranian nukes.'

"The only possible conclusion is that a government that consistently lies is not believable. …

"Having served Washington's propaganda purposes, the downed Malaysian airliner … [has] dropped out of the news even though [the] stor[y] remain[s] completely and totally unresolved.

"Washington's stooge government in Ukraine has not released the records of communications between Ukrainian air traffic control and Malaysian flight 17, and Washington has not released the photos from its satellite which was directly overhead at the time of the airliner's demise. We can safely and conclusively conclude from this purposeful withholding of evidence that the evidence does not support Washington's and Kiev's propaganda.

"We can also safely and conclusively conclude that the Western media's sudden disinterest in the unresolved story and failure to demand the evidence kept secret by Washington and Kiev is in keeping with the Western media's role as a Ministry of Propaganda.

"In other words, Washington and its presstitutes are protecting the lie that Washington and its media vassals successfully spread around the world and have used as the basis for further sanctions that escalate the conflict with Russia. Washington could not possibly make it clearer that Washington intends to escalate, not defuse, the conflict that Washington alone orchestrated."[24]

More War Preparations

Regardless of the lack of evidence for the U.S. claims of Russian involvement and responsibility in the Malaysia Airlines disaster, Commander Philip Breedlove has begun

---

chemical attack and blame Assad. When the Washington-orchestrated attack happened on schedule, … Russia and China did not fall for it. And neither did the British Parliament." (Paul Craig Roberts, "If Nuclear War Doesn't Exterminate Us Ebola Virus Might," August 1, 2014; http://www.paulcraigroberts.org/2014/08/01/nuclear-war-doesnt-exterminate-us-ebola-virus-might-paul-craig-roberts/)

[24] Paul Craig Roberts, "US Intelligence: No Evidence Russia Did It," July 23, 2014 (http://www.paulcraigroberts.org/2014/07/23/us-intelligence-evidence-russia-paul-craig-roberts/) and "Ukraine Crisis Continues," August 20, 2014 (http://www.paulcraigroberts.org/2014/08/20/ukraine-crisis-continues-paul-craig-roberts/).

to organize NATO forces as if for a war against Russia. Breedlove is currently pursuing plans for stockpiling war material[25] on Russia's borders so that NATO troops can strike at Russia within mere hours or minutes of an order.

Meanwhile, U.S. Senate bill 2277, the "Russian Aggression Prevention Act of 2014" (which some believe is worded like a declaration of war against Russia), is on the table of the Foreign Relations Committee. The bill includes an ultimatum to the Kremlin demanding that Russia entirely abandon Crimea within seven days of the Act's passage, and it also calls for permanently basing NATO forces near Russia's borders (in Poland, Estonia, Lithuania, and Latvia).

Most significantly, the bill calls for assigning Ukraine the status of an "ally of the U.S.," which will effectively open the door to more direct U.S. military involvement in Ukraine. This involvement could include not only the suppression of the ethnic Russians, the so-called separatists, in eastern Ukraine, but also a direct engagement with Russia should President Putin step in to protect the ethnic Russians in Ukraine. (The bill thus offers the Obama administration an end-run around the hotly disputed question of bringing Ukraine into NATO. The proposed alliance would provide a justification for military actions in Ukraine by U.S. troops regardless of whether or not Ukraine becomes a partner nation in NATO.)

President Obama, too, has been quick to lead the E.U. into imposing yet another round of economic sanctions to punish Russia for its supposed involvement in the downing of MH-17, in spite of the many voices calling for caution. Former U.S. Representative Ron Paul likens the embarrassment of Washington's baseless allegations against the separatists to that of the accusations against President Assad a year ago — both of which scenarios threatened to instigate a major war with Russia:

> "Tuesday the US government admitted it had been bluffing about its certainty that Russia was behind the downing of Malaysian Air Flight MH-17 over Ukraine. This dramatic turn of events started with State Department Spokeswoman Marie Harf claiming Monday that the State Department's certainty of Russian involvement in the apparent downing of the plane was primarily based on "social media" evidence. That means with a likely budget of more than $100 billion, the US Intelligence Community is making decisions that may involve global nuclear war based on people's Tweets and YouTubes! ...

> "[Harf claimed:] 'Based on open information which is basically common sense, right — we know where it was fired from, we know who has this weapon.'

> "Who needs evidence — it's 'common sense'! Right? ...

25   Cf. "NATO Poland Base May Be Prepared For Blitz Against Russia," RT, July 24, 2014; http://rt.com/news/175292-nato-poland-supply-base/

"It was a near exact replay of similar US government claims about Syria's Assad using chemical weapons last year. That time, Secretary of State Kerry claimed dozens of times on television that 'we know' Assad fired the chemicals into the village. Yet the US Intelligence Community refused to sign off on his claims and the Obama Administration was forced to release what it called a 'Government Assessment' rather than the standard Intelligence Community consensus assessment. ...

"*Sanctions are acts of war*. ... Why are they risking a major war with Russia to deny people in Ukraine the right to self-determination? ... [L]et's not forget that this whole crisis started with the US-sponsored coup against Ukraine's elected president back in February. The US escalates while it demands that Russia de-escalate. How about all sides de-escalate?"[26]

Europe in the Path of Destruction

It is feared that such groundless and provocative *acts of war*, as Ron Paul calls them, will naturally *lead to war* if the West continues on its present course, for when the next war comes, there will be no winner. The whole world is certain to lose that war, and one of the first losers in a NATO war against Russia is likely to be Europe.

Gabor Steingart, the editor of *Handelsblatt* (Germany's most respected financial newspaper, similar to our *Wall Street Journal*), recently published a signed editorial berating the German press for parroting U.S. propaganda. He also denounced what he believes to be the madness of America's policy toward Russia as a recipe for war. Steingart writes:

"Every war is accompanied by a kind of mental mobilization: war fever. ... German journalism has switched from level-headed

Gabor Steingart, the editor of Germany's most respected financial newspaper, published an Incisive editorial denouncing the madness of the U.S. and EU's policy of demonizing Russia and of purposely stoking up a "war fever" in the West.

to agitated in a matter of weeks. The spectrum of opinions has been narrowed to the field of vision of a sniper scope. Newspapers we thought to be all about thoughts and ideas now march in lock-step with politicians in their calls for sanctions against Russia's President Putin. ...

---

[26] Ron Paul, "On Malaysian Crash, Obama's Case Against Russia Disintegrates," July 23, 2014 (http://ronpaulinstitute.org/archives/featured-articles/2014/july/23/on-malaysian-crash-obamas-case-against-russia-disintegrates.aspx), and "Why Won't Obama Just Leave Ukraine Alone?", August 3, 2014 (emphasis added), Ron Paul Institute for Peace and Prosperity (http://ronpaulinstitute.org/archives/featured-articles/2014/august/03/why-won-t-obama-just-leave-ukraine-alone.aspx).

19

"The politics of escalation show that Europe sorely lacks a realistic goal. It's a different thing in the US. Threats and posturing are simply part of the election preparations. When Hillary Clinton compares Putin with Hitler, she does so only to appeal to the Republican vote, *i.e.* people who do not own a passport. For many of them, Hitler is the only foreigner they know, which is why Adolf Putin is a very welcome fictitious campaign effigy. In this respect, Clinton and Obama have a realistic goal: to appeal to the people, to win elections, to win another Democratic presidency.

[German Chancellor] Angela Merkel can hardly claim these mitigating circumstances for herself. Geography forces every German Chancellor to be a bit more serious. As neighbors of Russia, as part of the European community bound in destiny, as recipient of energy and supplier of this and that, we Germans have a clearly more vital interest in stability and communication. We cannot afford to look at Russia through the eyes of the American Tea Party. …

"The verbalists are back and their headquarters are in Washington D.C. But nobody is forcing us to kowtow to their orders. Following this lead — even if calculatingly and somewhat reluctantly as in the case of Merkel — does not protect the German people, but may well endanger it. This fact remains [*i.e.*, would remain] a fact even if it was not the Americans but the Russians who were responsible for the original damage in the Crimean and in eastern Ukraine. [*Editor's note*: In other words, the German people would be endangered by following America's lead even if it had been a Russian-backed coup that toppled the Ukrainian government and ignited a civil war in Ukraine. But given America's role in fomenting the present tensions over Ukraine, it is all the more dangerous for Germany to follow the United States' lead in antagonizing Germany's near neighbor Russia.] …

"It does not make sense to just follow the strategically idea-less Obama. Everyone can see how he and Putin are driving like in a dream directly towards a sign which reads: Dead End. … Demonizing Putin is not a policy. It is an alibi for the lack thereof. He advises condensing conflicts, *i.e.* to make them smaller, shrink them, and then distill them into a solution. But at the present moment (and for a long time before) America is doing the opposite. All conflicts are escalated. The attack of a terror group named Al Qaida is turned into a global campaign against Islam. Iraq is bombed using dubious justifications. Then the US Air Force flies on to Afghanistan and Pakistan. The relationship to the Islamic world can safely be considered damaged.

"If the West had judged the then US government which marched into

20

Iraq without a resolution by the UN and without proof of the existence of 'WMDs' [weapons of mass destruction] *by the same standards as Putin today, then George W. Bush would have immediately been banned from entering the EU. The foreign investments of Warren Buffett should have been frozen, the export of vehicles of the brands GM, Ford, and Chrysler banned.*

"The American tendency to verbal and then to military escalation, the isolation, demonization, and attacking of enemies, has not proven effective. The last successful major military action the US conducted was the Normandy landing. Everything else — Korea, Vietnam, Iraq, and Afghanistan — was a clear failure. *Moving NATO units towards the Polish border [with Russia] and thinking about arming Ukraine are continuations of a policy of relying on military means in the absence of diplomacy*.

"This policy of running your head against the wall – and doing so exactly where the wall is the thickest – just gives you a headache and not much else. … [More prudent statesmen such as former German Chancellor Willie] Brandt and [Egon] Bahr have never reached for the tool of economic sanctions. They knew why: There are no recorded cases in which countries under sanctions apologized for their behavior and were obedient ever after. On the contrary: collective movements start in support of the sanctioned, as is the case today In Russia. The country was hardly ever more unified behind their president than now. This could almost lead you to think that the rabble-rousers of the West are on the payroll of the Russian secret service."[27]

---

[27]   Gabor Steingart, "The West on the Wrong Path," *Handelsblatt*, August 8, 2014 (emphasis added); http://www.handelsblatt.com/meinung/kommentare/essay-in-englisch-the-west-on-the-wrong-path/10308406.html

On September 28-30, 1939, German troops paraded through Warsaw after breaking through the Polish border defenses only four weeks earlier on September 1st. Adolf Hitler had carefully prepared the way for his troops with a propaganda campaign directed at his own people, leading many of the German people to desire a war with their European neighbors.

Chapter 2
War Fever: Important Historical Precedents

In the Nuremburg Trials of 1946, there came to light a series of Gestapo-organized "false-flag"[28] terrorist actions which Hitler had used to set the stage for his invasion of Poland in 1939. By staging attacks on an assortment of German facilities along the Polish border — a pair of railway stations, a forest service station, a customs house, and other sites — Hitler created the appearance of Polish aggression against Germany, which he was then able to use as a justification for the invasion of Poland.

One of these attacks took place at the German radio station in Gleiwitz (in Upper Silesia, then part of Germany, now being Gliwice, in southern Poland), made to look as though it had been the work of Polish saboteurs. For added credibility, it was decided that this incident would involve a known "Polish rebel," who could be killed in the course of the "insurgency."

On the day before the incident, the Gestapo arrested a 41-year-old German Silesian farmer (whom they had selected from police files as being a well-known local Polish sympathizer), and then drugged him into semi-consciousness.

At about 8 p.m. the next day, a band of SS soldiers (some wearing Polish military uniforms, others dressed as Polish rogues) overran the Gleiwitz radio station, and beat up the three (German) employees manning the station. After broadcasting a brief anti-German invective in Polish, they dragged the farmer from their car to the entrance of the station and shot him in the back of the head.

To all appearances, the Polish sympathizer had been killed while attacking the station, and his corpse was acknowledged by both the police and the press as proof of Polish involvement in the attack.

The Gleiwitz incident took place on the day before Hitler's invasion of Poland. About a week before the incident, Hitler had told his generals,

> "I will provide a propagandistic *casus belli* [*i.e.*, an incident serving as justification for aggression]. Its credibility doesn't matter. The victor will not be asked whether he told the truth."[29]

(Hitler was right. The Gleiwitz myth persisted in Nazi Germany throughout the war years, without ever being seriously challenged.)

On the day following the Gleiwitz incident, after the invasion of Poland had begun,

---

[28] A "false-flag" operation is a deceptive action made to appear as though it had been carried out by a group or nation other than the real authors — thus, "under another flag."

[29] James J. Wirtz and Roy Godson, *Strategic Denial and Deception: The Twenty-First Century Challenge*, Transaction Publishers, 2002, ISBN 0-7658-0898-6, Google Print, p. 100 (http://books. google.ca/books?id=PzfQSITJTXkC&pg=PA100&ots=ouNc9JPz4y&dq=Gleiwitz+incident&as_ brr=3&sig=WZF91Hk_0WybC1nqbS8Ghw7nTzw&redir_esc=y#v=onepage&q=Gleiwitz%20 incident&f=false); and Bradley Lightbody, *The Second World War: Ambitions to Nemesis*, Routledge, 2004; ISBN 0-415-22405-5, Google Print, p. 39.

Hitler made a speech in the Reichstag citing the border attacks (which he himself had directed) as justification for Germany's aggression against Poland:

> "I can no longer find any willingness on the part of the Polish Government to conduct serious negotiations with us. ... [M]ore Polish atrocities... were again repeated last night. Recently in one night there were as many as twenty-one frontier incidents: last night there were fourteen, of which three were quite serious. I have, therefore, resolved to speak to Poland in the same language that Poland for months past has used toward us. ...

> "This night for the first time Polish regular soldiers fired on our own territory. Since 5:45 a.m. we have been returning the fire... I will continue this struggle, no matter against whom, until the safety of the Reich and its rights are secured."[30]

With that, the war was on — *but not without that careful preparation of the masses,* whose indignation had been skillfully fanned to fury against Germany's perceived foes.

The German people had been well schooled by Hitler in anticipation of the war. Throughout the months preceding the September 1, 1939 invasion of Poland, he had led the German newspapers and other politicians in accusing the Poles of conducting ethnic cleansings, murdering ethnic Germans living in Poland. The German army was thus in a sense propelled by the popular support which Hitler had garnered by demonizing Poland.

We may be inclined to think that such murderous and war-mongering things cannot happen today, or that our own government (whichever that may be) would not resort to such tactics. But on the contrary, since political leaders hardly dare to undertake any major endeavor without first attending to appearances and public perception, such deceptions are still very much with us. And nowhere is "perception management" (as the U.S. Department of Defense calls it)[31] so carefully attended to as in the employment of a nation's military.

The Power of Public Opinion

Whether for good purposes or bad, a war effort requires a consensus of minds. "More important than a standing army is an idea whose time has come."[32]

---

30   "Address by Adolf Hitler – September 1, 1939," Avalon Project of the Yale Law School; http://www.fcit. usf.edu/HOLOCAUST/resource/document/HITLER1.htm   Regarding details of the Gleiwitz incident, see "The Gleiwitz Incident: The 'First Man to Die' in the War," World War II Today; http://ww2today.com/the-gleiwitz-incident-and-the-first-man-to-die-in-world-war-ii

31   The Department of Defense gives this definition of *perception management*: "Actions to convey and/or deny selected information and indicators to foreign audiences to influence their emotions, motives, and objective reasoning as well as to intelligence systems and leaders at all levels to influence official estimates, ultimately resulting in foreign behaviors and official actions favorable to the originator's objectives. In various ways, perception management combines truth projection, operations security, cover and deception, and psychological operations." (Department of Defense Dictionary of Military and Associated Terms, Joint Publication 1-02, 12 April 2001, As Amended Through 17 December 2003; *Cf.* http://www.militaryfactory. com/dictionary/military-terms-defined.asp?term_id=4039)

32   Victor Hugo: "On résiste à l'invasion des armées; on ne résiste pas à l'invasion des idées." Histoire d'un Crime

Political leaders understand well this famous bit of advice from Victor Hugo. They know that their own citizens must be psychologically prepared for the burdens of a military campaign before their country goes to war.

There must be an impetus among the people, establishing a justification and appetite for war, in order to sustain a war effort. The enemies abroad are enough of a challenge in war time — no commander would care to fight a morale war on the home-front at the same time.

Our readers may recall how glowingly Senator Jeremiah Denton praised President Nixon for enduring the "hurricane of criticism [which] raged in the country and throughout the world"[33] in the final weeks of the Vietnam War. In December 1972, in what Denton called "the decisive moment of the war," Nixon holed himself up silently in the White House and, in spite of the anti-war protests, extended the U.S. military actions against North Vietnam until Hanoi would agree to the release of all POW's. Denton, the senior officer imprisoned in the "Hanoi Hilton," considered Nixon's efforts (particularly in the face of so much popular resistance) to be truly heroic.

Of course, not all war-time leaders are remembered so favorably as Denton regarded President Nixon — particularly when there is a question of the leaders having led their country into a war through fabricated pretenses. Adolf Hitler (an ever-present, easy target for historical condemnation) provided a classic example for us, above. But American history has its own share of similar black marks and questionable dealings.

A Varied Picture

The present writer is a proud citizen of the United States who takes no pleasure in finding fault with those who have led his country — and certainly there is no intention here to find fault with those who have served our country valiantly and honorably in the military, at the risk or expense of their lives. Giving our first and highest allegiance to the truth, however, we must be ready to accept the possibility of failings in our government's leadership (including its use of the armed forces), and be able to distinguish the country which we love from the particular leaders who happen to have served it at given times, more or less well.

Navy Captain Jeremiah Denton (who was a devout and outspoken Roman Catholic) addressed those who came to welcome and honor him at Clark Air Base in the Philippines shortly after his release from prison in Hanoi in February 1973. Denton described his seven years as a (tortured) POW in Vietnam in his book, *When Hell Was in Session*.

("The History of a Crime"; written 1852, published 1877), Conclusion, Ch. X.

[33] Sen. Jeremiah A. Denton, Jr., *When Hell Was in Session*, 1976, reprinted by Robert E. Hopper & Associates, Lake Wylie, South Carolina, 1982, p. 175.

John Weir of the Institute for Historical Review points out the importance of a candid appraisal of recent U.S. history, beginning with Pearl Harbor's catapulting the country into the Second World War:[34]

"World War II [was] the conflict by which America attained its superpower status. An important pillar of America's mythical self-image as a righteous superpower is the Pearl Harbor legend that the United States was minding its own business until the mad Japanese launched their unprovoked attack, dragging reluctant Americans into a terrible world war, and thereby obliging the United States to shoulder 'international responsibilities' as world judge, philanthropist, and policeman.

"A broader understanding of the background to the Pearl Harbor attack, and especially President Roosevelt's secretive and unlawful efforts to provoke war, would go far toward shattering this popular legend…. For as long as the myth of the United States as the reluctant geopolitical messiah endures, Americans will resist viewing this century's history with candor…."[35]

President Abraham Lincoln was not above recognizing our failings as a nation, and he officially declared a day of repentance and reparation "for our national sins." His proclamation of the National Fast Day of 1863 is well worth reading. It remains a stirring example to us all:

"By the President of the United States of America. A Proclamation.

"Whereas, the Senate of the United States, devoutly recognizing the Supreme Authority and just Government of Almighty God, in all the affairs of men and of nations, has, by a resolution, requested the President to designate and set apart a day for National prayer and humiliation.

"And whereas it is the duty of nations as well as of men, to own their dependence upon the overruling power of God, to confess their sins and transgressions, in humble sorrow, yet with assured hope that genuine repentance will lead to mercy and pardon; and to recognize the sublime truth, announced in the Holy Scriptures and proven by all history, that those nations only are blessed whose God is the Lord.

"And, insomuch as we know that, by His divine law, nations like individuals are subjected to punishments and chastisements in this world, may we not justly fear that the awful calamity of civil war, which now desolates the land, may be but a punishment, inflicted upon us, for our presumptuous sins, to the needful end of our national reformation as a whole

---

[34] See Appendix I in this book for a discussion of the Pearl Harbor controversy.

[35] John Weir, "Exonerating Pearl Harbor's Scapegoats," *The Journal of Historical Review*, Vol. 16, No. 6, Nov.-Dec. 1997, p. 40; http://www.ihr.org/jhr/v16/v16n6p35_Weir.html

President John F. Kennedy meets with the Joint Chiefs of Staff (JCS) in the White House Cabinet Room on May 27, 1961. In March 1962, the Joint Chiefs of Staff presented to the Kennedy administration a series of proposals called Operation Northwoods, signed by JCS Chairman, General Lyman Lemnitzer (seated 2nd from left, between President Kennedy and Air Force General Curtis LeMay). The plan called for the CIA or other U.S. operatives to commit "false-flag" terrorist acts such as bombings and hijackings — both real killings, and also merely simulated attacks which would be presented through the media as if they had been real events — in American cities and military installations. Contrived "evidence" would then be presented implicating the Cuban government, and creating public support for a U.S. invasion of Cuba.

The plan called for the United States to actively develop a "Communist Cuban terror campaign in the Miami area, in other Florida cities, and even in Washington. ... The desired resultant from the execution of this plan would be to place the United States in the apparent position of suffering grievances from a rash and irresponsible government of Cuba and to develop an international image of a Cuban threat to peace in the Western Hemisphere." (See the 12-page document, declassified in 1997, in PDF format in the National Security Archive, http://www2.gwu.edu/~nsarchiv/news/20010430/northwoods.pdf)

This U.S. Government plan for the murder and deception of its own people received the official authorization of the Joint Chiefs of Staff, but then was flatly rejected by President Kennedy.

People? We have been the recipients of the choicest bounties of Heaven. We have been preserved, these many years, in peace and prosperity. We have grown in numbers, wealth and power, as no other nation has ever grown. But we have forgotten God. We have forgotten the gracious hand which preserved us in peace, and multiplied and enriched and strengthened us; and we have vainly imagined, in the deceitfulness of our hearts, that all these

27

blessings were produced by some superior wisdom and virtue of our own. Intoxicated with unbroken success, we have become too self-sufficient to feel the necessity of redeeming and preserving grace, too proud to pray to the God that made us!

"It behooves us then, to humble ourselves before the offended Power, to confess our national sins, and to pray for clemency and forgiveness.

"Now, therefore, in compliance with the request, and fully concurring in the views of the Senate, I do, by this my proclamation, designate and set apart Thursday, the 30th day of April, 1863, as a day of national humiliation, fasting, and prayer. And I do hereby request all the People to abstain, on that day, from their ordinary secular pursuits, and to unite, at their several places of public worship and their respective homes, in keeping the day holy to the Lord, and devoted to the humble discharge of the religious duties proper to that solemn occasion.

"All this being done, in sincerity and truth, let us then rest humbly in the hope authorized by the Divine teachings, that the united cry of the Nation will be heard on high, and answered with blessings, no less than the pardon of our national sins, and the restoration of our now divided and suffering Country, to its former happy condition of unity and peace.

"In witness whereof, I have hereunto set my hand and caused the seal of the United States to be affixed.

"Done at the City of Washington, this thirtieth day of March, in the year of our Lord one thousand eight hundred and sixty-three, and of the Independence of the United States the eighty seventh.

"By the President: Abraham Lincoln"[36]

Kennedy and Operation Northwoods

We Americans can also be justly proud of the many men of principle who have served our country in public office. President John F. Kennedy is a pointed example, particularly in juxtaposition to the questions attached to President Roosevelt's role in the disaster at Pearl Harbor.

President Kennedy, to his enduring credit, refused his Joint Chiefs of Staff's proposal (called Operation Northwoods) to carry out acts of terrorism against both Cuban refugees and American citizens in Florida which could be blamed on Fidel Castro in order to secure domestic and global support for a U.S. invasion of Cuba.

---

[36] President Abraham Lincoln, "Proclamation Appointing a National Fast Day," March 30, 1863; http://www.abrahamlincolnonline.org/lincoln/speeches/fast.htm

Historian Robert Dallek summarizes the too-little-known facts of the matter:

"Kennedy couldn't ignore the pressure to end Communist control of Cuba. He wasn't ready to tolerate Castro's government and its avowed objective of exporting socialism to other Western Hemisphere countries. He was willing to entertain suggestions for ending Castro's rule as long as the Cuban regime demonstrably provoked a U.S. military response or as long as Washington's role could remain concealed. To meet Kennedy's criteria, the Joint Chiefs endorsed a madcap plan called Operation Northwoods. It proposed carrying out terrorist acts against Cuban exiles in Miami and blaming them on Castro, including physically attacking the exiles and possibly destroying a boat loaded with Cubans escaping their homeland. The plan also contemplated terrorist strikes elsewhere in Florida, in hopes of boosting support domestically and around the world for a U.S. invasion. Kennedy said no."[37]

A Sad Pattern

Professor Joseph Ellis of Williams College notes:

"When you study how the U.S. goes to war, there is a prevalent though not perfect pattern. The triggering event is often a sudden crisis that galvanizes popular opinion and becomes the immediate occasion for military intervention, but subsequently is exposed as a misguided perception or outright fabrication."[38]

Professor Ellis refers here, among other things, to the manner in which President James Polk found (or created) a *casus belli* for the Mexican War of 1846 (a war which he is believed to have greatly desired); to the instigation of the Spanish-American War of 1898 under President William McKinley over the still-mysterious sinking of the USS *Maine* in Havana Harbor; and to the United States' entry into the Vietnam War in 1964 in response to a fictitious incident in the Gulf of Tonkin. (See Appendix II for a fuller explanation of this war-triggering incident.)

Tragically, in recent years we have seen what appears to be a series of just such watershed events — some clearly contrived and even murderous — which have actually been used to create a consensus for war in the U.S. and other Western nations against various targeted nations:

---

[37] Robert Dallek, "JFK vs. The Military," September 10, 2013, *The Atlantic*; http://www.theatlantic.com/magazine/archive/2013/08/jfk-vs-the-military/309496/ *Cf.* U.S. Joint Chiefs of Staff, "Justification for US Military Intervention in Cuba (TS[Top-Secret])," U.S. Department of Defense, 13 March 1962; PDF file of National Security Archive at the George Washington University Gelman Library, Washington, D.C., at http://www2.gwu.edu/~nsarchiv/news/20010430/doc1.pdf

[38] Joseph J. Ellis, "American Wars Often Start with a Lie: The American Way of War May Surprise You," *Chicago Tribune*, July 7, 2014; http://articles.chicagotribune.com/2014-07-07/opinion/ct-war-obama-history-0707-20140707_1_military-intervention-vietnam-war-world-trade-center

- The supposed massacres taking place in Kosovo in 1999, which served as a pretext for the NATO bombing of Yugoslavia.[39]
- The 9/11 attacks on the World Trade Center (which are by no means satisfactorily explained by the official reports and mainstream media accounts)[40] which led to the U.S. invasion of Afghanistan in October 2001; and
- The ploy of blaming President Assad for the August 2013 sarin gas attack on a Syrian village, which would have given President Obama his much-sought opportunity to attack Syria, had it not been discovered that the attack was actually launched by the U.S.-backed insurgents in order to spur direct U.S. military action against Assad.[41]

The list could go on. Professor Ellis continues, adding a discussion of the events leading up to the U.S. invasion of Iraq in 2003:

> "This pattern is not perfect. ... American military intervention in Iraq, however, fits the pattern perfectly. As we watch the enormous U.S. investment in blood and treasure over the last 11 years dissolve in Iraq, history requires that we remember the reasons we went to war, [and] why they were untrue.
>
> President George W. Bush ... argued that Iraqi leader Saddam Hussein possessed weapons of mass destruction, including a nuclear capacity, and that there were clear connections between Iraq and the al-Qaeda terrorists responsible for the 9/11 attacks on the World Trade Center and the Pentagon. Both claims were concocted.

---

[39]   Cf. Blokhin Timur and Vukotic Iovanna, "NATO's War against Yugoslavia Was Based on Lies," Global Research, March 24, 2014; http://www.globalresearch.ca/nato-s-war-against-yugoslavia-was-based-on-lies/32302

About this forgery-based public relations campaign, Herbert Foerstel writes: "Within the print media, the *Washington Post* led the drum-beat for war, spinning a tabloid tale of a new holocaust in the Serbian province of Kosovo, perpetrated by the new Hitler, Slobodan Milosevic, president of Yugoslavia and Serbia, its largest republic. No matter that these parallels were contradicted by the facts: Milosevic came to power through elections, not a putsch [i.e., a violent overthrow of the government]; Serbia represented no threat to any of its neighbors; and casualties in the Kosovo conflict prior to NATO bombing had been the lowest in any civil war in modern history. President Clinton, seeking a defining event on which to end his tarnished administration, surfed [or 'rode,' as Americans would say] the tabloid waves into a brutal, purposeless war. It was another great story that flowed seamlessly from the Lewinsky scandal." (Herbert N. Foerstel, *From Watergate to Monicagate: Ten Controversies in Modern Journalism and Media*, Greenwood Press, Westport, Connecticut, 2001, p. 132; http://books.google.ca/s?id=HorHFYH0NsoC&pg=PA132&lpg=PA132&dq=Who+tied+the+lewinski+scandal+to+the+Kosovo+war%3F&source=bl&ots=fbLzfRczrr&sig=MkE8rIfEEy2EyPqFuwngtmSojxs&hl=en&ei=qx47TYXbKY36swOA_bzVAw&sa=X&oi=book_result&ct=result&redir_esc=y#v=onepage&q&f=false)

[40]   See the summary of information presented by the Society of Architects and Engineers for 9/11 Truth, http://architectsandengineersfor911truth.org/

[41]   *Cf.* Pete Papaherakles, "Syria Innocent," *American Free Press*, April 28, 2014, http://americanfreepress.net/?p=17005 (this article draws heavily upon the book *The Red Line and the Rat Line* by Seymour Hersh, Pulitzer Prize recipient); and Richard Walker, "Iraqis Uncover Sarin Gas Lab With Ties to U.S. Ally in Syria," *American Free Press*, December 4, 2013, http://americanfreepress.net/?p=11173

"But the dark shadow of 9/11 hung ominously over all deliberations in that moment, so the CIA bent the evidence to fit the fabrication, a cowed Congress went along, and the bulk of the American media endorsed the deception. Dissent became unfashionable."

What Weapons of Mass Destruction?

As Professor Ellis suggests, a review of the events leading up to the U.S. invasion of Iraq in 2003 is in order.

Beginning more than a year before the invasion of Iraq, President Bush and other senior members of his administration made repeated claims that Iraq was engaged in producing weapons of mass destruction (WMDs), and in fact was already in possession of chemical, biological and even nuclear weapons. Asserting without qualification that Iraq definitely possessed WMDs, the Bush administration insisted that Saddam Hussein's regime constituted a grave and imminent threat to the United States and to the world at large.

Yet at the same time, U.S. and foreign intelligence agencies, the International Atomic Energy Agency (IAEA), and other groups, concurred in affirming that Iraq's nuclear program had ended in 1991 following the first Gulf War, and was never reconstituted. These agencies confirmed repeatedly (through almost 400 inspections between November 2002 and the time of the invasion in March 2003)[42] that Iraq had destroyed its chemical weapons stockpile in 1991 and its biological weapons in 1991 and 1992.

On January 29, 2002, President George W. Bush said in his State of the Union address:

> "Iraq continues to flaunt its hostility toward America and to support terror. The Iraqi regime has plotted to develop anthrax, and nerve gas, and nuclear weapons for over a decade. ... By seeking weapons of mass destruction, these regimes pose a grave and growing danger.

> "We'll be deliberate, yet time is not on our side. I will not wait on events, while dangers gather. I will not stand by, as peril draws closer and closer. The United States of America will not permit the world's most dangerous regimes to threaten us with the world's most destructive weapons."[43]

On February 13, 2002, Knight Ridder Newspapers reported:

> "President Bush has decided to oust Iraqi leader Saddam Hussein from power and ordered the CIA, the Pentagon and other agencies to devise a combination of military, diplomatic and covert steps to achieve that goal, senior U.S. officials said Tuesday.

---

[42]   *Cf.* Charles Hanley, "No Violations at Iraqi Sites of Concern," Associated Press, January 18, 2003; http://www.apnewsarchive.com/2003/No-Violations-at-Iraqi-Sites-of-Concern/id-d72cb596688193b82dde1b259428d8af

[43]   Transcript archived at http://georgewbush-whitehouse.archives.gov/stateoftheunion/2002/

"No military strike is imminent, but Bush has concluded that Saddam and his nuclear, chemical and biological weapons programs are such a threat to U.S. security that the Iraqi dictator must be removed, even if U.S. allies do not help, said the officials, who all spoke on condition of anonymity.

"'This is not an argument about whether to get rid of Saddam Hussein. That debate is over. This is ... how you do it,' a senior administration official said in an interview with Knight Ridder."[44]

But on the contrary, on March 15, 2002, the British Cabinet Office's Joint Intelligence Committee insisted that there was no verifiable evidence of a WMD program in Iraq (reported in 2004 in London's *Daily Telegraph*):

"The latest Joint Intelligence Committee assessment, dated Friday, March 15 [2002], said information on Saddam's weapons of mass destruction was 'sporadic and patchy… There is no intelligence on any biological agent production facilities.'"[45]

On March 24, 2002, Vice President Dick Cheney appeared on CNN's *Late Edition*, saying:

"This is a man of great evil, as the President said. And he is actively pursuing nuclear weapons at this time…"[46]

On August 26, 2002, Vice President Dick Cheney addressed the Veterans of Foreign Wars 103rd National Convention in Nashville, Tennessee, claiming:

"But we now know that Saddam has resumed his efforts to acquire nuclear weapons. Among other sources, we've gotten this from the firsthand testimony of defectors — including Saddam's own son-in-law, who was subsequently murdered at Saddam's direction. Many of us are convinced that Saddam will acquire nuclear weapons fairly soon.

"Simply stated, there is no doubt that Saddam Hussein now has weapons of mass destruction. There is no doubt he is amassing them to use against our friends, against our allies, and against us…

"As President Bush has said, time is not on our side. Deliverable weapons of mass destruction in the hands of a terror network, or a murderous dictator, or the two working together, constitutes as grave a threat as can be

44   Warren P. Strobel and John Walcott , "Bush Has Decided to Overthrow Hussein," Knight Ridder Newspapers, February 13, 2002, McClatchy Washington Bureau, http://www.mcclatchydc.com/2002/02/13/16310/bush-has-decided-to-overthrow.html

45   Michael Smith, "Failure Is Not an Option, But It Doesn't Mean They Will Avoid It," *Daily Telegraph*, November 18, 2004; http://www.telegraph.co.uk/news/worldnews/middleeast/iraq/1472042/Failure-is-not-an-option-but-it-doesnt-mean-they-will-avoid-it.html?mobile=basic

46   Transcript archived at http://www.leadingtowar.com/PDFsources_claims_noweapons1/2002_03_24_whitehouse.pdf

imagined. The risks of inaction are far greater than the risk of action…"[47]

But on the contrary, as the *Washington Post* reported (in 2006, three years after the invasion):

"[On Aug. 26, 2002, Cheney said:] 'We now know that Saddam has resumed his efforts to acquire nuclear weapons… Among other sources, we've gotten this from firsthand testimony from defectors, including Saddam's own son-in-law.'

"[Cheney's statement] was a reference to Hussein Kamel, who had managed Iraq's special weapons programs before defecting in 1995 to Jordan. But Saddam Hussein lured Kamel back to Iraq, and he was killed in February 1996, so Kamel could not have sourced what U.S. officials 'now know.'

"And Kamel's testimony, after defecting, was the reverse of Cheney's description. In one of many debriefings by U.S., Jordanian, and U.N. officials, Kamel said on Aug. 22, 1995, that Iraq's uranium enrichment programs had not resumed after halting at the start of the Gulf War in 1991."[48]

And further to the contrary, in September 2002, former chief UN Special Commission in Iraq [UNSCOM] weapons inspector Scott Ritter challenged Cheney's claim by pointing out a key part of Kamel's testimony:

"Throughout his interview with UNSCOM, Hussein Kamel reiterated his main point — that nothing was left. 'All chemical weapons were destroyed,' he said. 'I ordered destruction of all chemical weapons. All weapons — biological, chemical, missile, nuclear — were destroyed. There is not a single missile left.'"[49]

On September 7, 2002, President George W. Bush addressed the press at Camp David:

"I would remind you that when the inspectors … went into Iraq … a report came out of the Atomic — the IAEA — that they were six months away from developing a weapon. I don't know what more evidence we need."[50]

47   Transcript archived at http://www.leadingtowar.com/PDFsources_claims_noweapons1/2002_08_26_whitehouse.pdf

48   Barton Gellman and Walter Pincus, "Depiction of Threat Outgrew Supporting Evidence," *Washington Post*, August 10, 2003; http://www.washingtonpost.com/wp-dyn/content/article/2006/06/12/AR2006061200932.html

49   Scott Ritter, "Cheney's Warped Perspective on the Need to Attack Iraq," *Chicago Tribune*, September 10, 2002, http://articles.chicagotribune.com/2002-09-10/news/0209100286_1_chemical-weapons-saddam-hussein-hussein-kamal

50   Archived at http://www.leadingtowar.com/PDFsources_claims_noweapons1/2002_09_07_whithouse.pdf

But on the contrary, on September 27, 2002, the *Washington Times* reported:

"The International Atomic Energy Agency says that a report cited by President Bush as evidence that Iraq in 1998 was 'six months away' from developing a nuclear weapon does not exist.

"'There's never been a report like that issued from this agency,' Mark Gwozdecky, the IAEA's chief spokesman, said yesterday in a telephone interview from the agency's headquarters in Vienna, Austria. ...

"'There are no indications that there remains in Iraq any physical capability for the production of weapon-usable nuclear material of any practical significance,' IAEA Director-General Mohammed Elbaradei wrote in a report to U.N. Secretary-General Kofi Annan.

"Mr. Gwozdecky said... 'I don't know where they have determined that Iraq has retained this much weaponization capability because when we left in December '98 we had concluded that we had neutralized their nuclear-weapons program. We had confiscated their fissile material. We had destroyed all their key buildings and equipment,' he said.

"Mr. Gwozdecky said there is no evidence about Saddam's nuclear capability right now — either through his organization, other agencies, or any government."[51]

On September 8, 2002, Secretary of State Colin Powell claimed on *Fox News Sunday*:

"There is no doubt that he has chemical weapons stocks... There's no question that he has these weapons. But even more importantly, he is striving to do even more, to get even more."[52]

On September 12, 2002, President George W. Bush addressed the United Nations General Assembly, claiming:

"U.N. inspectors believe Iraq has produced two to four times the amount of biological agents it declared, and has failed to account for more than three metric tons of material that could be used to produce biological weapons. Right now, Iraq is expanding and improving facilities that were used for the production of biological weapons.

"United Nations' inspections also revealed that Iraq likely maintains stockpiles of VX, mustard and other chemical agents, and that the regime is rebuilding and expanding facilities capable of producing chemical

---

[51]   Joseph Curl, "Agency Disavows Report on Iraq Arms," *Washington Times*, September 27, 2002, http://www.washingtontimes.com/news/2002/sep/27/20020927-091051-4501r/?page=all

[52]   Transcript archived at http://www.leadingtowar.com/PDFsources_claims_noweapons1/2002_09_08_Fox_State.pdf

weapons..."With every step the Iraqi regime takes toward gaining and deploying the most terrible weapons, our own options to confront that regime will narrow. And if an emboldened regime were to supply these weapons to terrorist allies, then the attacks of September the 11th would be a prelude to far greater horrors."[53]

On September 18, 2002, Secretary of Defense Donald Rumsfeld testified before the House Armed Services Committee hearing:

"[Hussein's] regime has amassed large clandestine stocks of biological weapons, including anthrax and botulism toxin and possibly smallpox. His regime has amassed large stockpiles of chemical weapons, including VX and sarin and mustard gas."[54]

On September 20, 2002, Vice President Dick Cheney spoke at a GOP fundraiser in Casper, Wyoming:

"We now have irrefutable evidence that he has once again set up and reconstituted his program to take uranium, to enrich it to sufficiently high grade, so that it will function as the base material as a nuclear weapon."[55]

But on the contrary, in September 2002, the Defense Intelligence Agency (DIA) issued a report (declassified by the Department of Defense on June 9, 2003) stating:

"There is no reliable information on whether Iraq is producing and stockpiling chemical weapons, or where Iraq has — or will — establish its chemical warfare agent production facilities."[56]

On September 26, 2002, Secretary of Defense Donald Rumsfeld told the press in the Pentagon Press Room:

"We know they have weapons of mass destruction. We know they have active programs. There isn't any debate about it."[57]

On September 26, 2002, President Bush addressed the press in the White House Rose Garden:

"The danger to our country is grave... The Iraqi regime possesses biological and chemical weapons. The Iraqi regime is building the facilities necessary to make more biological and chemical weapons.

---

[53] Transcript archived at http://www.leadingtowar.com/PDFsources_claims_noweapons1/2002_09_12_whitehouse.pdf

[54] Transcript archived at http://www.leadingtowar.com/PDFsources_claims_noweapons1/2002_09_18_CNN.pdf

[55] Cited by U.S. Congress in House Resolution 625, "Censuring the President and Vice President," August 4, 2007, http://www.gpo.gov/fdsys/pkg/BILLS-110hres625ih/html/BILLS-110hres625ih.htm

[56] Archived at http://www.leadingtowar.com/PDFsources_claims_noweapons1/2002_09_Sept_DIA.pdf

[57] Transcript archived at http://www.leadingtowar.com/PDFsources_claims_noweapons1/2002_09_26_defense.pdf?transcriptid=3669

"According to the British government, the Iraqi regime could launch a biological or chemical attack in as little as 45 minutes, after the order were given."[58]

On October 7, 2002, President Bush outlined the Iraqi threat at the Cincinnati Museum Center:

"Saddam Hussein is a homicidal dictator who is addicted to weapons of mass destruction.

"We agree that the Iraqi dictator must not be permitted to threaten America and the world with horrible poisons, and diseases, and gasses, and atomic weapons. …

"The evidence indicates that Iraq is reconstituting its nuclear weapons program. … If the Iraqi regime is able to produce, buy, or steal an amount of highly enriched uranium a little larger than a single softball, it could have a nuclear weapon in less than a year.

"America must not ignore the threat gathering against us. Facing clear evidence of peril, we cannot wait for the final proof, the smoking gun, that could come in the form of a mushroom cloud."[59]

On December 3, 2002, Secretary of Defense Donald Rumsfeld spoke in the Pentagon Press Room, claiming:

"The United States knows that Iraq has weapons of mass destruction. The U.K. knows that they have weapons of mass destruction. Any country on the face of the earth with an active intelligence program knows that Iraq has weapons of mass destruction."[60]

But on the contrary, on December 8, 2002, in compliance with U.N. Security Council Resolution 1441, Iraq submitted a complete declaration of all aspects of its programs to develop chemical, biological, and nuclear weapons, as reported by the *New York Times*:

"Iraq today delivered a 12,000-page declaration on banned weapons to the United Nations, meeting a Security Council deadline with more than 24 hours to spare. Officials said the documents confirmed, in rebuttal of American and British claims, that Saddam Hussein's government had no weapons of mass destruction and no current programs to develop them."[61]

---

58   Transcript archived at http://www.leadingtowar.com/PDFsources_claims_noweapons1/2002_09_26_whitehouse.pdf

59   Transcript archived at http://www.leadingtowar.com/PDFsources_claims_noweapons1/2002_10_07_whitehouse.pdf

60   Transcript archived at http://www.leadingtowar.com/PDFsources_claims_noweapons1/2002_12_03_defenseDept.pdf

61   John F. Burns with David E. Sanger, "Threats and Responses: Arms Inspections; Iraq Says Report to the

Secretary of State Colin Powell (pictured here displaying a model vial of anthrax) went before the United Nations Security Council on February 5, 2003, in order (as he told the council members) "to share with you what the United States knows about Iraq's weapons of mass destruction, as well as Iraq's involvement in terrorism."

The U.S. media, led by the *Washington Post* and the *New York Times*, praised Powell's speech as irrefutable, and accepted unquestioningly Powell's warning to the Security Council that it would place itself "in danger of irrelevance" by failing to endorse a U.S.-led invasion of Iraq.

In the meantime, the information on which this pivotal speech was based has been thoroughly discredited. Powell's own words describing Iraq, as characterized by a policy of "evasion and deception," have now come to be generally applied to Powell's speech itself.

Both Powell and his speech-writer, U.S. Army Col. Lawrence Wilkerson, have disavowed that speech, which served a key role in establishing the case for invading Iraq. In Wilkerson's words, "It was the lowest point in my professional and personal life. I wish I had not been involved in it." (Watch at http://www.youtube.com/watch?v=wX9Ywf1jI2Q. *Cf.* "Former Aide: Powell WMD Speech 'Lowest Point In My Life,'" CNN, http://www.cnn.com/2005/WORLD/meast/08/19/powell.un/)

Describing the intelligence reports on which the speech was based as both "politicized" and "wrong at its roots," Wilkerson regrets having added momentum to the drive toward invading Iraq. He salves his conscience, however, with his estimation that war with Iraq was already a given at that time: "I don't believe that the hype about that presentation having been the ultimate presentation, as it were, that led us to war with Iraq. George W. Bush, Dick Cheney and others had decided to go to war with Iraq long before Colin Powell gave that presentation." ("Decade After Iraq WMD Speech at UN, Ex-Powell Aide Lawrence Wilkerson Debates Author Norman Solomon", *Democracy Now!*, February 6, 2013, http://www.democracynow.org/2013/2/6/decade_after_iraq_wmd_speech_at)

On February 5, 2003, Secretary of State Colin Powell addressed the United Nations Security Council:

> "[E]very statement I make today is backed up by sources, solid sources. These are not [mere] assertions....

U.N. Shows No Banned Arms," *New York Times*, December 8, 2002, http://www.nytimes.com/2002/12/08/world/threats-responses-arms-inspections-iraq-says-report-un-shows-no-banned-arms.html

"One of the most worrisome things that emerges from the thick intelligence file we have on Iraq's biological weapons is the existence of mobile production facilities used to make biological agents....

"Our conservative estimate is that Iraq today has a stockpile of between 100 and 500 tons of chemical weapons agent. That is enough agent to fill 16,000 battlefield rockets."[62]

On February 11, 2003, CIA Director George Tenet testified before the Senate Select Committee on Intelligence:

"I think we will find caches of weapons of mass destruction, absolutely."[63]

But on the contrary, on March 7, 2003, on the basis of months of U.N. weapons inspections, International Atomic Energy Agency (IAEA) Director General Mohamed ElBaradei reported in a speech to the United Nations:

"[T]here is no indication of resumed nuclear activities in those buildings that were identified through the use of satellite imagery as being reconstructed or newly erected since 1998, nor any indication of nuclear-related prohibited activities at any inspected sites. ...

"After three months of intrusive inspections, we have to date found no evidence or plausible indication of the revival of a nuclear weapon program in Iraq....

"I should note that in the past three weeks, possibly as a result of ever-increasing pressure by the international community, Iraq has been forthcoming in its cooperation, particularly with regard to the conduct of private interviews and in making available evidence that could contribute to the resolution of matters of IAEA concern..."[64]

On March 16, 2003, Vice President Dick Cheney said on NBC News' *Meet the Press*:

"*We believe [Hussein] has, in fact, reconstituted nuclear weapons*. I think Mr. ElBaradei frankly is wrong."[65]

On March 17, 2003, President Bush delivered an Address to the Nation, stating:

"Intelligence gathered by this and other governments leaves no doubt

---

[62]   Transcript archived at http://www.leadingtowar.com/PDFsources_claims_noweapons2/2003_02_05_Statedept.pdf

[63]   Congressional Report archived at http://www.leadingtowar.com/PDFsources_claims_noweapons2/2003_02_11_TenetSenate.pdf

[64]   Transcript archived at http://www.leadingtowar.com/PDFsources_claims_noweapons2/2003_03_07_CNN.pdf

[65]   Emphasis added. Transcript archived at http://www.leadingtowar.com/PDFsources_claims_noweapons2/2003_03_16_NBCmtp.pdf

that the Iraq regime continues to possess and conceal some of the most lethal weapons ever devised.

"The danger is clear: using chemical, biological, or, one day, nuclear weapons, obtained with the help of Iraq, the terrorists could fulfill their stated ambition and kill thousands or hundreds of thousands of innocent people in our country, or any other."[66]

But on the contrary, as *The Washington Post* reported on March 18, 2003:

"As the Bush administration prepares to attack Iraq this week, it is doing so on the basis of a number of allegations against Iraqi President Saddam Hussein that have been challenged — and in some cases disproved — by the United Nations, European governments, and even U.S. intelligence reports.

"For months, President Bush and his top lieutenants have produced a long list of Iraqi offenses, culminating Sunday [March 16] with ***Vice President Cheney's assertion that Iraq has 'reconstituted nuclear weapons*** .' Previously, administration officials have tied Hussein to al Qaeda, to the Sept. 11, 2001, terrorist attacks, and to an aggressive production of biological and chemical weapons. Bush reiterated many of these charges in his address to the nation last night.

"But these assertions are hotly disputed. Some of the administration's evidence — such as Bush's assertion that Iraq sought to purchase uranium — has been refuted by subsequent discoveries.

"Earlier this month, ElBaradei said information about Iraqi efforts to buy uranium were based on fabricated documents."[67]

On March 19, 2003, disregarding both international law and the findings of numerous intelligence agencies, as well as widespread international protests, President Bush launched the planned U.S. invasion of Iraq.

The ensuing war caused the violent deaths of more than 4,000 American servicemen, as well as (directly or indirectly) the deaths of an estimated 500,000 Iraqis.

A further consequence of the war has been that Iraq and much of the Middle East have succumbed to a brutal sectarian chaos, while a still-growing radical Islamic element, inflamed against the West, spreads bloodshed and turmoil over ever increasing regions.

In the end, after many months of exhaustive investigations, no stockpiles of chemical, biological, or nuclear weapons were found, and neither was there found any evidence

---

[66]   Transcript archived at http://www.leadingtowar.com/PDFsources_claims_noweapons2/2003_03_17_ whitehouse.pdf

[67]   Walter Pincus and Dana Milbank, "Bush Clings to Dubious Allegations about Iraq," *Washington Post*, March 18, 2003, emphasis added. Cited in the Congressional Record, Volume 149, Number 43 (Tuesday, March 18, 2003) http://www.gpo.gov/fdsys/pkg/CREC-2003-03-18/html/CREC-2003-03-18-pt1-PgH1927-5.htm

of active WMD programs.

By May 14, 2003, less than two months after the invasion, Bush administration officials had begun to deny having made their previous claims. Defense Secretary Donald Rumsfeld answered Senators' questions at the hearing of the Defense Subcommittee of the Senate Appropriations Committee, stating:

"Senator, I don't believe anyone that I know in the administration ever said that Iraq had nuclear weapons. So the statement I think you read, which — that we've warned of potential nuclear capability and weapons and materials in the hands of terrorists, in terms of their having them now, I don't know anyone who suggested that that was the case."[68]

After more than 18 months, the exhaustive investigations and searches for weapons of mass destruction in Iraq were abandoned. Dr. David Kay, who led the CIA-appointed task force (called the Iraq Survey Group, ISG), testified before the Senate Armed Services Committee in a January 28, 2004 hearing about the investigations, admitting:

"It turns out that we were all wrong, probably in my judgment, and that is most disturbing."[69]

Kay's conclusion was expounded in an *Associated Press* article:

"In his final word, the CIA's top weapons inspector in Iraq said Monday that the hunt for weapons of mass destruction has 'gone as far as feasible' and has found nothing, closing an investigation into the purported programs of Saddam Hussein that were used to justify the 2003 invasion."[70]

In the ISG's final report, issued on September 30, 2004, it is stated:

"Saddam [Hussein] ended the nuclear program in 1991 following the Gulf War. ISG found no evidence to suggest concerted efforts to restart the program.

"While a small number of old, abandoned chemical munitions have been discovered, ISG judges that Iraq unilaterally destroyed its undeclared chemical weapons stockpile in 1991. There are no credible indications that Baghdad resumed production of chemical munitions thereafter."[71]

Greg Thielmann (the former Director of the Strategic, Proliferation, and Military Affairs Office for the U.S. State Department's Bureau of Intelligence and Research

---

[68]   Transcript archived at http://www.leadingtowar.com/PDFsources_claims_noweapons2/2003_05_14_defense_appro.pdf

[69]   Transcript archived at http://www.cnn.com/2004/US/01/28/kay.transcript/

[70]   "CIA's Final Report: No WMD Found in Iraq," Associated Press, April 25, 2005, http://www.nbcnews.com/id/7634313/ns/world_news-mideast_n_africa/t/cias-final-report-no-wmd-found-iraq/

[71]   Final Report archived at http://www.leadingtowar.com/PDFsources_claims_noweapons2/2004_09_30_globalsecurity.pdf

— *i.e.*, Colin Powell's intelligence bureau, whose input Powell disregarded[72]), in an interview on CBS' *60 Minutes*, stated in regard to Powell's allegation that Iraq had posed an imminent threat to the U.S.:

"I think it didn't even constitute an imminent threat to its neighbors at the time we went to war. … The main problem was that the senior administration officials have what I call faith-based intelligence. They knew what they wanted the intelligence to show. They were really blind and deaf to any kind of countervailing information the intelligence community would produce."[73]

In October 2004, a lengthy *New York Times* article examined the intelligence debacle in great detail. Let's conclude this tragic timeline with a citation from that article:

"[A]s they studied raw intelligence reports, those involved in the Senate [Select Committee on Intelligence] investigation came to a sickening realization. 'We kept looking at the intelligence and saying, "My God, there's nothing here,"' one official recalled."[74]

The Presidents Who Cried "Wolf!"

Former Reagan administration Cabinet Member Paul Craig Roberts offers this withering assessment of the present U.S. government's credibility:

"It is clear as day that the US government has lost credibility among large segments of the American population as well as abroad. Increasingly, Americans do not believe their government or the media that lies for the government. This is why the print and TV media are on the decline, making it easier for the CIA to buy the media to serve its agendas.[75]

"Where shall we begin? Clinton's lies about Serbia and Kosovo? George W. Bush's lies about Saddam Hussein's weapons of mass destruction? Obama's lies about Gaddafi and Assad's use of chemical weapons? The

---

[72]   *Cf.* Jonathan Schwarz, "Lie After Lie After Lie: What Colin Powell Knew Ten Years Ago Today and What He Said," *Huffington Post*, February 5, 2013, http://www.huffingtonpost.com/jonathan-schwarz/colin-powell-wmd-iraq-war_b_2624620.html

[73]   Reported in Rebecca Leung, "The Man Who Knew: Ex-Powell Aide Says Saddam-Weapons Threat Was Overstated," CBS News, October 14, 2003, http://www.cbsnews.com/news/the-man-who-knew-14-10-2003/

[74]   David Barstow, William J. Broad, and Jeff Gerth, "How the White House Embraced Disputed Arms Intelligence," *New York Times*, October 3, 2004, http://www.nytimes.com/2004/10/03/international/middleeast/03tube.html?pagewanted=print&

[75]   An example of this which has recently come to light involves Germany, where public opinion is notably more positive towards Russia than in other countries. Udo Ulfkotte, a former editor of one of Germany's largest mainstream newspapers, *Frankfurter Allgemeine Zeitung*, has published a best-selling book revealing that for decades, the CIA has been paying German media members to spin the news in a way that supports U.S. interests. *Cf.* "Top German Editor: CIA Bribing Journalists," *Russia Insider*, October 3, 2014; http://russia-insider.com/en/tv_politics_media_watch/2014/10/10/06-31-52pm/top_german_editor_cia_bribing_journalists

lies about Iranian nukes? Obama's lies about Ukraine? The demonization of Putin?

"Or shall we go back to the official lies about President John F. Kennedy's assassination? Or Martin Luther King's? Tonkin Gulf? The USS Liberty? Pearl Harbor? "Remember the Maine"? Or the granddaddy of them all — 9/11?[76]

"Try to come up with one important event about which the US government did not lie.

"My Ph.D. dissertation chairman, Warren Nutter, … taught his students that democracy requires trust between the government and the people. Clearly, the government does not trust the American people. Washington pursues hidden agendas that it advances by deceiving the American people.

"The first observant and patriotic citizens who warned us of the deceptions practiced by our government were dismissed as 'anti-American.' Patriotism became defined as 'belief in the government's word,' as British Prime Minister Cameron reiterated the other day. Today skeptics who utilize free speech are defined by Homeland Security as 'domestic extremists.' …

"As Warren Nutter taught, our democracy only works when the government's agenda is openly revealed and consistent with American principles. When the government lies in order to orchestrate wars that benefit special interests, the government breaks trust with the people and becomes arbitrary, dictatorial, and unaccountable. And when the media prefers money to truth, the government gets away with it."[77]

A dark picture, indeed — and yet the lesson should be clear enough. Our Lady of Fatima's Message grows more urgent with each passing day. Against such deceptions, lies, and official war propaganda, "only She can help [us]," as She Herself said at Fatima.

Unless and until Our Lady deigns to intervene and stop this deadly spiral toward Armageddon (which She will do when Her main Fatima request is obeyed, as She promised at Fatima and Tuy), we can expect these pretexts for war to continue to be created until the powers-that-be get all the wars that they so desire.

But as Our Lady of Fatima warned, if Her requests are not heeded in time, "various nations will be annihilated." These same powers-that-be may also get a war which becomes so big that it destroys virtually all of us, including them.

---

[76] See also Dr. Roberts' fuller discussion of this topic in Paul Craig Roberts, "9/11 After 13 Years," September 10, 2014; http://www.paulcraigroberts.org/2014/09/10/911-13-years-paul-craig-roberts/

[77] Paul Craig Roberts, "Ebola Update," October 11, 2014; http://www.paulcraigroberts.org/2014/10/11/ebola-update-paul-craig-roberts/

The wreckage of MH-17's left wing shows more evidence of an air-to-air assault by a military jet against the civilian plane. Clearly visible across the top of the wing is the trace of a grazing bullet, along a trajectory which extends directly toward the plane's cockpit.

The SU-25 jet fighter's 30mm cannons fire alternating rounds of anti-tank incendiary shells and splinter-explosive shells. These latter explosive shells are designed to cause numerous massive explosions inside the object fired upon (in most cases, a tank). If used against a commercial aircraft at high altitude, the explosions would increase the pressure inside the cabin to breaking-point levels, causing the aircraft to burst like a balloon.

This scenario coincides precisely with the destruction of MH-17, whose wreckage was scattered across fields covering an area of 20 square kilometers. The largely intact fragments of the plane's rear sections were broken apart in midair along the weaker points of construction, apparently not through a missile strike, but through extreme internal air pressure.

(Photo credit: Jeroen Akkermans/RTL-4 Nieuws/Netherlands)

A mushroom cloud rises above Nagasaki, Japan on August 9, 1945, signaling the horrific deaths of tens of thousands of urban Japanese civilians from the atomic blast and radiation. Beyond those who suffered this sudden and unprovided death (such as we pray to be delivered from in the Litany of the Saints), many more perished over time in the greatest torments imaginable, in the ensuing fires and from radiation burns. In all, the two atomic bombs dropped on Japan in 1945 took nearly two hundred thousand lives, but those bombs are dwarfed by the destructive power of today's thermonuclear weapons, 17,000 of which fill the arsenals of the world.

CHAPTER 3
Nuclear War: A Growing Prospect

We would all do well to consider what kind of a fate our world leaders seem to be preparing for us. As Paul Craig Roberts has repeatedly stressed, the next war will be an apocalypse for most of the world's population:

"The kind of reckless lies and transparent propaganda ... being conducted against Russia by the US and UK governments and Ministries of Propaganda, a.k.a. [also known as] the "Western media," ... in order to demonize Putin and Russia ... [have] no other purpose than to drive the world to a war that no one can win. ... The Western elites and governments are not merely totally corrupt, they are insane. As I have previously written, don't expect to live much longer."[78]

"The lies that the Obama regime and Western presstitute media are hurling at President Putin are even more blatantly false that the lies Washington used against Saddam Hussein, Gaddafi, Assad, the Taliban, and Iran, and the lies are far more reckless. Russia has a nuclear arsenal as large as Washington's, and Russia is very much aware that for 13 years Washington's lies and demonizations of countries have been the preludes to launching military attacks on the countries."[79]

"If Obama believes what he told the press, he is utterly disinformed by his advisors. If he doesn't believe the crude propaganda that he speaks, he is consciously leading the drive to war with Russia which probably means war with China as well and the end of us all. ... Russia and China are not Iraq, Libya, or Afghanistan. War with Russia will be nuclear."[80]

"The Western media consists of idiots who are enabling Washington's drive toward war and the extermination of life on earth. ... I am concerned about the crisis that Washington has orchestrated, because I believe it is leading to war, which will be nuclear. Are you ready to be destroyed over Washington's lies about one Malaysian airliner? I am convinced that Washington is behind the destruction of MH-17, because Washington's propaganda show was already ready and was instantly in performance. That

[78]   Paul Craig Roberts, "War Is Coming," July 28, 2014; http://www.paulcraigroberts.org/2014/07/28/war-coming-paul-craig-roberts/

[79]   Paul Craig Roberts, "The West's Reckless Rush Towards War With Russia," July 31, 2014; http://www.paulcraigroberts.org/2014/07/31/wests-reckless-rush-towards-war-russia/

[80]   Paul Craig Roberts, "If Nuclear War Doesn't Exterminate Us Ebola Virus Might," August 1, 2014; http://www.paulcraigroberts.org/2014/08/01/nuclear-war-doesnt-exterminate-us-ebola-virus-might-paul-craig-roberts/

Washington is responsible is the reason that Washington will not release its satellite photos of the area during the moment of the airliner's destruction. That Washington is responsible is the reason that Washington replies to Russian hard evidence with lies and propaganda. … The propagandized people in the West have no idea of the fate toward which their demented governments are driving them. … Unless the world reins in the demented criminals in Washington, the world has signed its own death warrant."[81]

A Murderer from the Beginning

Since the days of the Manhattan Project, when scientists in the U.S. raced those in Hitler's Germany to develop the first atomic bomb, willful murder has been at the heart of every nuclear weapons program.

Is it permissible to do something evil in the hope of bringing about some good effect (*e.g.* trying to hasten the end of a war by slaughtering innocent people)? Never. Is it ever permissible to directly take innocent lives? No, not even in times of war. To indiscriminately target an entire city for destruction — homes, schools, hospitals, everything and everyone in the city — is a murderous act, and never justifiable.

Catholic moral theology describes the circumstances in which a foreseeable **unintended** evil effect may justifiably follow from an action. The first two conditions demanded by the principle of "two-fold effect" (or "double effect") are that *the action itself must not be morally evil* (such as the direct taking of innocent lives) and that *the evil effect must not be directly intended* (such as purposely choosing urban population centers as targets for military strikes).

We would do well to ask ourselves whether we can even *threaten* to do such forbidden and murderous acts without being guilty of oppressing the weak, the defenseless, and the poor. Such bullying cries to Heaven to be thoroughly humbled by Heaven and by man.

It has long been the policy of various Western nations to consider nuclear armaments as *defensive* weapons, whose mere possession would deter foreign aggressors. The supposition has been that by pointing some of these murderous weapons at a rival nation's major cities, a nation would provide a sort of "nuclear shield" to its own cities. At the same time, the threat of "mutually assured destruction" would supposedly prevent any country from actually employing its nuclear weapons. Paul Craig Roberts explains:

> "Prior to the Bush and Obama regimes, every previous US president went to great efforts to avoid telegraphing any nuclear threat. US war doctrine was careful to keep nuclear weapons limited to retaliation in the event the US suffered a nuclear attack. The purpose of nuclear forces was to prevent the use of such weapons."[82]

[81] Paul Craig Roberts, "If Nuclear War Doesn't Exterminate Us Ebola Virus Might," August 1, 2014; http://www.paulcraigroberts.org/2014/08/01/nuclear-war-doesnt-exterminate-us-ebola-virus-might-paul-craig-roberts/

[82] Paul Craig Roberts, "Washington Threatens The World," August 8, 2014; http://www.paulcraigroberts.org/2014/08/08/washington-threatens-world-paul-craig-roberts/

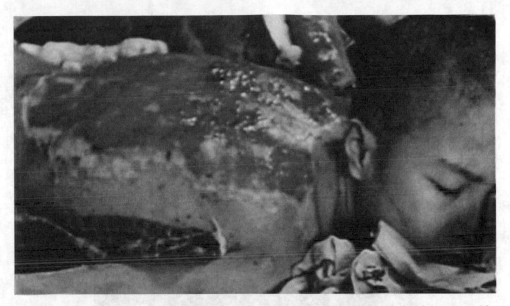

In a 1962 Department of Defense report on "The Effects of Nuclear Weapons" which was read by President Kennedy, radiation burns were acknowledged to be so severe as to cause hemorrhaging, leading to "anemia and death. ... If death does not take place in the first few days after a large dose of radiation, bacterial invasion of the blood stream usually occurs and the patient dies of infection." (*Cf.* the 1964 Revised Edition Internet Archive eBook at https://archive.org/details/TheEffectsOfNuclearWeapons). Only after repeated demands to his Joint Chiefs of Staff was the President shown the nation's blueprint for nuclear war — the Joint Strategic Capabilities Plan. To his horror, JFK saw that the U.S. military planned to drop 170 atomic and nuclear bombs on Moscow alone, and to destroy every major Soviet, Chinese, and Eastern European city. The anticipated death toll was in the hundreds of millions. Visibly sickened by the formal briefing on the plan, the President said, "And we call ourselves the human race!" He later remarked to one of his aides: "These brass hats have one great advantage. If we do what they want us to do, none of us will be alive later to tell them that they were wrong."

John F. Kennedy, for instance, was convinced that a nuclear war would be "the final failure" of world leaders, and that a nuclear exchange would indeed bring mutually assured destruction to the nations involved. The President's military advisors, however, were for the most part more concerned about not letting the United States' technological advantage[83] over Russia at that time slip away from them, than they were concerned with averting Armageddon. From the beginning of his presidency, Kennedy struggled to rein in his military Chiefs of Staff lest they precipitate a nuclear war against Russia. Historian Robert Dallek writes:

> "The stalemate in the Korean War had frustrated military chiefs and left them inclined to use atomic bombs to ensure victory, as General Douglas MacArthur had proposed. ... [T]he Joint Chiefs believed the United States

---

[83]   Though Moscow already had the hydrogen bomb at that time, Russian missile technologies lagged, giving Moscow no effective means of delivering the bombs. President Kennedy's advisors argued that it would be best to pre-emptively crush Russia while they could still do so with little risk to the American population.

President John F. Kennedy poses with the U.S. Joint Chiefs of Staff after a meeting on January 15, 1963. Standing next to the President are U.S.A.F. Gen. Thomas Power (2ⁿᵈ from right) and Gen. Curtis LeMay (3ʳᵈ from left), both of whom avidly urged President Kennedy to take advantage of the temporary technological advantage which the U.S. then had over Russia. The best course, they insisted, would be to use the United States' nuclear arsenal to bomb the Russian nation into submission — military and civilian population alike.

could fight such a [nuclear] conflict and win. … They regarded Kennedy as reluctant to put the nation's nuclear advantage to use and thus resisted ceding him exclusive control over decisions about a first strike. …

"[Air Force] General [Thomas] Power was openly opposed to limiting the use of America's ultimate weapons. 'Why are you so concerned with saving their lives?' he asked the lead author of a Rand study that counseled against attacking Soviet cities [with nuclear warheads] at the outset of a war. 'The whole idea is to kill the bastards…. At the end of the war, if there are two Americans and one Russian, we win.' Even Curtis LeMay, Power's superior, described him as 'not stable' and a 'sadist.'

"The 54-year-old LeMay, known as 'Old Iron Pants,' wasn't much different. He shared his subordinate's faith in the untrammeled use of air power to defend the nation's security. The burly, cigar-chomping caricature of a general believed the United States had no choice but to bomb its foes

The desolate remains of a once crowded and bustling region of Tokyo, after the fire-bombing carried out on the night of March 9, 1945 under USAF Major General Curtis LeMay. An estimated 100,000 people lost their lives that night as 267,000 buildings burned to the ground in the single deadliest air raid of World War II.

into submission. In World War II, LeMay had been the principal architect of the incendiary attacks by B-29 heavy bombers that destroyed a large swath of Tokyo and killed about 100,000 Japanese — and, he was convinced, shortened the war. LeMay had no qualms about striking at enemy cities, where civilians would pay for their governments' misjudgment in picking a fight with the United States."[84]

Kennedy's own reasoning was very different, and (particularly after the Bay of Pigs incident) he began purposely to avoid as much as possible taking any advice from the CIA, the Pentagon, and the State Department. Speaking about nuclear weapons with Secretary of Defense Robert McNamara and other military chiefs a few weeks after the conclusion of the Cuban Missile Crisis, the President asked: "What good are they? You can't use them as a first weapon yourself. They are only good for deterring ... I don't see quite why we're building as many as we're building."[85]

The United States' New War Doctrine

The basis of modern-day international law dates back to the 17th-century Treaty

---

[84]   Robert Dallek, "JFK vs. The Military," *The Atlantic*, September 10, 2013; http://www.theatlantic.com/magazine/archive/2013/08/jfk-vs-the-military/309496/

[85]   *Ibid.*

of Westphalia,[86] which simultaneously brought to an end the Thirty Years War in the Holy Roman Empire and the Eighty Years War between Spain and the Dutch Republic. At the heart of the political order established by this Peace of Westphalia in 1648 (an order which has endured throughout the past three and a half centuries, until the recent concessions toward globalization) is the concept of *sovereign states* having the right to conduct their domestic affairs without interference from other nations.

In terms of military actions, this regard toward mutual sovereignties required that nations refrain from any warlike incursions against the rights and territories of their neighbors. A nation could, of course, use its own military force to meet another nation's unjust military aggression, but there could be no justification of a first attack. Civil laws reflect the same principle, as we all know — the suspicion that someone is meditating evil toward us is not enough to warrant our shooting him first.

The series of pre-emptive wars of aggression waged by the United States throughout the past decade, set in motion by the 9/11 (2001) attacks against the New York City World Trade Center, followed a policy change introduced in 2002 by President George W. Bush. By 2003, Vice President Dick Cheney was already able to boast, "If there is anyone in the world today who doubts the seriousness of the Bush Doctrine, I would urge that person to consider the fate of the Taliban in Afghanistan, and of Saddam Hussein's regime in Iraq."

The infamous "Bush Doctrine," on the other hand, implemented in the year 2002, goes directly against this principle of non-interference and non-aggression, and likewise against the longstanding view of nuclear weapons as purely defensive armaments.

---

[86] Actually a series of treaties signed between May and October 1648 in Osnabrück and Münster, building upon the Peace of Augsburg of 1555. Though the Westphalian Peace was denounced at the time by Pope Innocent X for its inroads against the rights of the Church, it nevertheless included some sound principles. Sadly, even these last vestiges of a Christian social order are today being discarded.

In the aftermath of the 9/11 attacks in 2001, President George W. Bush announced a new direction for U.S. military policy that would include pre-emptive attack strategies, including *first-strike nuclear* attacks,[87] against any country.

Far more galling, however, even than that initial declaration of the Bush Doctrine, was President Obama's recent reiteration of it in his West Point Military Academy graduation address. Internationally acclaimed journalist John Pilger writes:

> "Delivering his 'state of the world' address at the graduation ceremony of those who 'will take American leadership' across the world, Obama said, 'I believe in American exceptionalism with every fiber of my being. ... The United States will use military force, unilaterally if necessary, when our core interests demand it. International opinion matters, but America will never ask permission...'
>
> "In repudiating international law and the rights of independent nations, the American president claims a divinity based on the might of his 'indispensable nation.' It is a familiar message of imperial impunity...."[88]

No longer does the U.S. acknowledge the burden of demonstrable proof of outside aggression before responding with military force, and no longer does it consider nuclear warheads merely *retaliatory* weapons, supposedly never to be used first.

U.S. military strategists seem convinced that a nuclear war can be won by the nation which *strikes first* and which so thoroughly *devastates its enemy* that it need not fear retaliation. U.S. military planners and government leaders alike are thus thinking openly now not in terms of *deterring* nuclear war, but of *"winning"* a nuclear war (as if there could be a winner).

The diabolic and murderous doctrine of total war which has infected Western civilization since the American Civil War, viewing civilian non-combatants as legitimate military targets, is now in full bloom. The pre-emptive genocide of entire nations has come to be considered a justifiable military strategy.

A Discarded Treaty

Part of the new "Bush Doctrine" as announced in 2002 was the abandonment of the

---

[87] The National Security Strategy of the United States (or "Bush Doctrine"), published on September 17, 2002, states: "[T]he first duty of the United States Government [is] to protect the American people and American interests. It is an enduring American principle that this duty obligates the government to anticipate and counter threats, **using all elements of national power**, before the threats can do grave damage. The greater the threat, the greater is the risk of inaction — and the more compelling the case for taking anticipatory action to defend ourselves, even if uncertainty remains as to the time and place of the enemy's attack. ... To forestall or prevent such hostile acts by our adversaries, the United States will, if necessary, act preemptively in exercising our inherent right of self-defense." (White House website archives, emphasis added; http://georgewbush-whitehouse.archives.gov/nsc/nss/2006/sectionV.html)

[88] John Pilger, "The Return of George Orwell and Big Brother's War on Palestine, Ukraine and the Truth," johnpilger.com: The Films and Journalism of John Pilger, July 11, 2014; http://johnpilger.com/articles/the-return-of-george-orwell-and-big-brothers-war-on-palestine-ukraine-and-truth

Anti-Ballistic Missile (ABM) Treaty of 1972. According to the terms[89] of that treaty, the United States and the Soviet Union agreed to limit the number of their anti-ballistic missile systems (which are used to defend against missile-delivered nuclear weapons).

What had been the purpose of such a treaty? Why had it been considered so important to limit the number of these *defensive* missiles, which are aimed not at cities, but rather at incoming nuclear-armed missiles, in defense of cities? *Because the prospect of "mutually assured destruction" would be nullified by a web of ABM bases surrounding a country, and each country would then be under tremendous pressure to launch a first strike against its enemies before it suffers a first strike from them!*

A country possessing a ring of ABM bases around its enemy nation would have the capability of attacking that nation without being attacked in turn, since the ABM missiles would supposedly be able to intercept any land-based retaliatory warheads before they left the country. In such a scenario, the danger of some country starting a nuclear war could not be greater.

Today, nuclear arsenals are maintained by the United States, Russia, China, India, Pakistan, Israel, North Korea, France, and the United Kingdom. Once the notion of mutually assured destruction is removed, virtually all life on earth would be hanging by a thread. Each of these rival nuclear powers would be under tremendous pressure to be the first to strike the others.

Many fear that we are almost there, thanks to the new U.S. war doctrine and the foreign policy of the past dozen years. By abandoning the ABM Treaty, the U.S. has opened the door to a strategic encirclement of Russia with ABM complexes, which would (supposedly) neutralize the threat of any retaliatory response from Russia to an American first strike.

Even more to be feared than the incentive that the U.S. will be under to start a nuclear war once these ABM complexes are in place, is the fact that Russia cannot and will not allow itself to be thus surrounded. Russia has an even more powerful incentive to launch a first-strike nuclear attack against the U.S. now, before more ABM complexes can be built.

A Disaster in Progress

Ever since its withdrawal from the ABM Treaty in June 2002, the U.S. has been aggressively pursuing just such a policy of encirclement against Russia. A number of ABM stations have already been built in Poland along the Russian border, and more are planned, beginning in Romania.[90] Coupled with the present volatility of Ukraine and the incessant media demonization of President Putin, John Pilger sees in this situation a recipe for World War III:

---

[89]   Under the terms of the treaty, each party was allowed only two ABM complexes, each of which could house no more than 100 anti-ballistic missiles.

[90]   *Cf.* Richard Cottrell, Rick Rozoff, and Bruce Gagnon, "US Plans 'First Strike' Nuclear Attack on Russia or China," *Global Research*, June 1, 2014; http://www.globalresearch.ca/us-plans-first-strike-attack-on-russia-or-china/5384799

"NATO's military encirclement has accelerated, along with US-orchestrated attacks on ethnic Russians in Ukraine. If Putin can be provoked into coming to their aid, his pre-ordained 'pariah' role will justify a NATO-run guerrilla war that is likely to spill into Russia itself."[91]

Not even President Bush, however, dared to authorize the development of a proposed Prompt Global Strike weapons system — a rapid-response delivery system employing hypersonic intercontinental-range missiles (supposedly armed only with conventional warheads) launched from submarines, aircraft, or space platforms, which will be able to strike a target anywhere in the world in less than an hour. President Bush rightly considered the program too dangerous, since it would be impossible for an enemy nation to know whether such ICBM-type missiles were carrying conventional or nuclear weapons. The deployment of these missiles would therefore trigger Russia's early warning system for nuclear attack, and provoke a nuclear war.

The Obama administration, however, has been less squeamish. Pursuing the goal of "full spectrum dominance" (the official term used by the Department of Defense in its May 30, 2000 document "Joint Vision 2020"),[92] the present administration is now aggressively developing the same Prompt Global Strike (PGS) system which was formerly rejected by President Bush.

The hypersonic weapons (traveling faster than the speed of sound) of this PGS system are considered by some to be the key to achieving the United States' desired "full spectrum" superiority in the seas, land, air, and space. In November 2011, the U.S. military's first Advanced Hypersonic Weapon (AHW) test took place, striking the Kwajalein Atoll from a launch base in Hawaii, more than 2,300 miles away, in fewer than 30 minutes. A second (failed) AHW test followed in August 2014 out of Alaska.

Thus at the present juncture, many things seem to indicate an intention for the U.S. to carry out a first-strike nuclear assault against Russia. Washington has withdrawn from the ABM treaty; has broken its assurances that NATO would not be expanded into the Baltics and Eastern Europe; has changed its war doctrine to include pre-emptive nuclear first-strikes; is establishing ABM missile bases on Russia's borders; and is

President Putin assures the West that Russia's military, backed by its nuclear arsenal, is ready to respond to any aggression.

91   John Pilger, "Break the Silence: A World War Is Beckoning," johnpilger.com: The Films and Journalism of John Pilger, May 13, 2014; http://johnpilger.com/articles/break-the-silence-a-world-war-is-beckoning

92   See the U.S. Department of Defense News article to this effect at http://www.defense.gov/news/newsarticle. aspx?id=45289. See also page 6 of the entire pdf document, "Joint Vision 2020," at http://www.pipr.co.uk/wp-content/uploads/2014/07/jv2020-2.pdf

developing a fast-strike delivery system. Certainly none of this has been lost on Russia.[93]

According to a report by Dr. Christof Lehmann of NSNBC International, "it is most likely and understandable" that Russia interprets NATO's Star Wars [advanced ABM system] deployment on its border as an "unofficial declaration of war."[94] Paul Craig Roberts also warns: "All of this is obviously directed at Russia, and the Russian government knows it. How long will Russia sit there waiting for Washington's first strike?"[95]

The obvious answer to that question should give us all the chills.

President Putin, in an interview on August 29, 2014, gave a pointed warning to foreign states, reminding them that Russia is one of the world's leading nuclear powers, and that it is prepared to use its nuclear arsenal to meet any aggression. "Russia's partners," he said, "should understand that it's best not to mess with us."[96]

As if to give confirmation to Putin's words, the Russian military has initiated a series of nuclear capabilities exercises. On September 8, two Russian strategic bombers flew over the northern Atlantic and Canada's northeast in a practice cruise missile attack on the United States.[97] Then on September 10, the Russian military conducted a test firing of its new Bulava intercontinental nuclear missile, which successfully struck its target in Russia's far east from a submarine launch in the White Sea. The 12-meter long, 40-ton missile has a range of 5000 miles and can carry 10 nuclear warheads.[98]

It is truly time for the West to do some soul-searching, and to listen to Our Lady of Fatima. We are being invited to do so, in the plainest terms.

On July 28, 2014, a Western international court in The Hague ruled that the Russian government had wrongly seized the Yukos oil company, and that Russia must pay the shareholders of the company $50 billion. Russia's response (aside from pointing out that the tribunal for private business disputes had no jurisdiction in the matter, and that its decision was politically biased by current events[99]) is very telling. When asked what Russia would do about the ruling, one of President Putin's close advisors replied: ***"There***

---

[93]   Watch a discussion by Russian journalists about U.S. plans for a first strike on Russia at http://financearmageddon.blogspot.co.uk/2014/07/official-warning-u-s-to-hit-russia-with.html, or read the transcript at http://www.globalresearch.ca/us-plans-first-strike-attack-on-russia-or-china/5384799

[94]   Cited in Richard Cottrell, "US Plans 'First Strike' Nuclear Attack on Russia or China," June 1, 2014, *Global Research*; http://www.globalresearch.ca/us-plans-first-strike-attack-on-russia-or-china/5384799

[95]   Paul Craig Roberts, "If Nuclear War Doesn't Exterminate Us Ebola Virus Might," August 1, 2014; http://www.paulcraigroberts.org/2014/08/01/nuclear-war-doesnt-exterminate-us-ebola-virus-might-paul-craig-roberts/

[96]   Alexei Anishchuk, "Don't Mess with Nuclear Russia, Putin Says," *Reuters*, August 29, 2014; http://www.reuters.com/article/2014/08/29/us-russia-putin-conflict-idUSKBN0GT1D420140829

[97]   *Cf.* Judi McLeod, "Russia Practicing Nuke Attacks on America from Canada," September 8, 2014, *Canada Free Press*; http://canadafreepress.com/index.php/article/65864?utm_source=CFP+Mailout&utm_campaign=03c3765c90-Call_to_Champions&utm_medium=email&utm_term=0_d8f503f036-03c3765c90-297718753

[98]   *Cf.* "Russia Successfully Tests Nuclear Missile, More Planned," *Reuters*, September 10, 2014,; http://freebeacon.com/national-security/russia-successfully-tests-nuclear-missile-more-planned/

[99]   Megan Davies, "Court Orders Russia to Pay $50 Billion for Seizing Yukos Assets," July 28, 2014; http://www.reuters.com/article/2014/07/28/us-russia-yukos-idUSKBN0FW0TP20140728

The pilot of the B-29 bomber which destroyed Hiroshima, Japan in 1945 with an atomic (fission) bomb signed this photo of the charred ruins, in which 135,000 lost their lives (totaling the immediate and consequent victims). Today's "nuclear" weapons are *fusion* bombs, hundreds of times more powerful and deadly than the "atomic" weapons used at the conclusion of World War II In a modern-day nuclear attack, hundreds of millions of people would perish all across a continent within a time span of only a few minutes.

is a war coming in Europe. Do you really think this ruling matters?"[100]

Where People Don't Matter

Justice Robert Jackson, who served as one of the chief prosecutors of Nazi war crimes at the Nuremberg Trials, called the unprovoked aggression of one country against another, "the supreme international crime, differing only from other war crimes in that it contains within itself the accumulated evil of the whole."[101]

It speaks volumes about our generation that there is so little outcry made about the epic public crimes taking place in our day. That we can also so easily overlook the consequent human suffering is an added rebuke to our already deadened sense of right and wrong.

Human tragedies on such a scale as have been witnessed in recent years, and which

100   Tyler Durden, "The Shocking Reason Putin Isn't Worried About The $50 Billion Yukos Ruling," *Zero Hedge*, July 28, 2014; http://www.zerohedge.com/news/2014-07-28/shocking-reason-putin-isnt-worried-about-50-billion-yukos-ruling

101   Bruce Broomhall, *International Justice and the International Criminal Court* (2 ed.), Oxford University Press, 2003, p. 46. ISBN 978-0-19-925600-6.

current events seem to be leading us toward, would hardly be possible without the complicity of the mass media, or without the willingness of people *en masse* to retreat from responsible thought. It would be difficult to say which party is the more guilty for the intellectual void which has settled over Western society today. John Pilger writes:

"A few years ago, Terry Eagleton, then professor of English literature at Manchester University, reckoned that 'for the first time in two centuries, there is no eminent British poet, playwright or novelist prepared to question the foundations of the western way of life.' No Shelley speaks for the poor, no Blake for utopian dreams, no Byron damns the corruption of the ruling class, no Thomas Carlyle and John Ruskin reveal the moral disaster of capitalism. William Morris, Oscar Wilde, HG Wells, George Bernard Shaw have no equivalents today. Harold Pinter was the last to raise his voice. Among the insistent voices of consumer-feminism, none echoes Virginia Woolf, who described 'the arts of dominating other people... of ruling, of killing, of acquiring land and capital." ...

"As Iraq is dismembered as a consequence of the Blair/Bush invasion, a *Guardian* headline declares: 'Toppling Saddam Was Right, But We Pulled Out Too Soon.' This ran across a prominent article on 13 June by a former Blair functionary, John McTernan, who also served Iraq's CIA-installed dictator Iyad Allawi. In calling for a repeat invasion of a country his former master helped destroy, he made no reference to the deaths of at least 700,000 people, the flight of four million refugees, and sectarian turmoil in a nation once proud of its communal tolerance. ...

"In a village in Afghanistan, inhabited by the poorest of the poor, I filmed Orifa, kneeling at the graves of her husband, Gul Ahmed (a carpet weaver), seven other members of her family (including six children), and two children who were killed in the adjacent house. A 'precision' 500-pound bomb fell directly on their small mud, stone, and straw house, leaving a crater 50 feet wide. ...

"The former US Secretary of State and aspiring President of the United States, Hillary Clinton, was recently on the BBC's '*Women's Hour*,' the quintessence of media respectability. The presenter, Jenni Murray, presented Clinton as a beacon of female achievement. She did not remind her listeners about Clinton's profanity that Afghanistan was invaded to 'liberate' women like Orifa. She asked Clinton nothing about her administration's terror campaign using drones to kill women, men and children. There was no mention of Clinton's idle threat, while campaigning to be the first female President, to 'eliminate' Iran, and nothing about her support for illegal mass surveillance and the pursuit of whistle-blowers.

"Murray did ask one finger-to-the-lips question. Had Clinton forgiven Monica Lewinsky for having an affair with her husband? 'Forgiveness is a choice,' said Clinton. 'For me, it was absolutely the right choice.' This recalled the 1990s and the years consumed by the Lewinsky 'scandal.' President Bill Clinton was then invading Haiti, and bombing the Balkans, Africa, and Iraq. He was also destroying the lives of Iraqi children; UNICEF reported the *deaths of half a million Iraqi infants under the age of five as a result of an embargo* led by the US and Britain. [Emphasis added.]

"The children were media unpeople, just as Hillary Clinton's victims in the invasions she supported and promoted — Afghanistan, Iraq, Yemen, Somalia — are media unpeople. Murray made no reference to them. …

"In politics as in journalism and the arts, it seems that dissent once tolerated in the 'mainstream' has regressed to a dissidence: a metaphoric underground. When I began a career in Britain's Fleet Street in the 1960s, it was acceptable to critique western power as a rapacious force. Read James Cameron's celebrated reports of the explosion of the Hydrogen bomb at Bikini [Pikinni] Atoll, the barbaric war in Korea and the American bombing of North Vietnam. Today's grand illusion is of an information age when, in truth, we live in a media age in which incessant corporate propaganda is insidious, contagious, effective, and liberal. …

"Tenure and patronage reward the guardians. On BBC Radio 4, Razia Iqbal interviewed Toni Morrison, the African-American Nobel Laureate. Morrison wondered why people were 'so angry' with Barack Obama, who was 'cool' and wished to build a 'strong economy and health care.' Morrison was proud to have talked on the phone with her hero, who had read one of her books and invited her to his inauguration.

"Neither she nor her interviewer mentioned Obama's seven wars, including his terror campaign by drone, in which whole families, their rescuers, and mourners have been murdered. What seemed to matter was that a 'finely spoken' man of color had risen to the commanding heights of power. …

"As the Iraqi city of Mosul fell to the jihadists of ISIS, Obama said, 'The American people made huge investments and sacrifices in order to give Iraqis the opportunity to chart a better destiny.' How 'cool' is that lie? …

"In February, the US mounted one of its 'color' coups against the elected government in Ukraine, exploiting genuine protests against corruption in Kiev. Obama's Assistant Secretary of State, Victoria Nuland, personally selected the leader of an 'interim government.' She nicknamed him 'Yats.' Vice President Joe Biden came to Kiev, as did CIA Director John Brennan. The shock troops of their putsch were Ukrainian fascists.

"For the first time since 1945, a neo-Nazi, openly anti-Semitic party controls key areas of state power in a European capital. No Western European leader has condemned this revival of fascism in the borderland through which Hitler's invading Nazis took millions of Russian lives. ...

"In reclaiming Crimea — which Nikita Kruschev illegally detached from Russia in 1954 — the Russians defended themselves as they have done for almost a century. More than 90 percent of the population of Crimea voted to return the territory to Russia. Crimea is the home of the Black Sea Fleet and its loss would mean life or death for the Russian Navy and a prize for NATO. ... [Meanwhile the Western media cooperates in] suppress[ing] news of the Kiev regime's war on its own people.

"A third of the population of Ukraine are Russian-speaking and bilingual. They have long sought a democratic federation that reflects Ukraine's ethnic diversity and is both autonomous and independent of Moscow. Most are neither 'separatists' nor 'rebels' but citizens who want to live securely in their homeland. Separatism is a reaction to the Kiev junta's attacks on them, causing as many as 110,000 (UN estimate) to flee across the border into Russia. Typically, they are traumatized women and children.

"Like Iraq's embargoed infants, and Afghanistan's 'liberated' women and girls, terrorized by the CIA's warlords, these ethnic people of Ukraine are media unpeople in the west, their suffering and the atrocities committed against them minimized, or suppressed. No sense of the scale of the regime's assault is reported in the mainstream western media. This is not unprecedented. Reading again Phillip Knightley's masterly *The First Casualty: The War Correspondent As Hero, Propagandist, and Mythmaker*,[102] I renewed my admiration for the Manchester *Guardian*'s Morgan Philips Price, the only western reporter to remain in Russia during the 1917 revolution and report the truth of a disastrous invasion by the western allies. Fair-minded and courageous, Philips Price alone disturbed what Knightley calls an anti-Russian 'dark silence' in the west.

"On 2 May, in Odessa, 41 ethnic Russians were burned alive in the trade union headquarters with police standing by. There is horrifying video

---

[102]   The book's title draws on the famous statement of American Senator Hiram Johnson in 1917, that "The first casualty when war comes, is truth." This 1975 classic about journalism as the purveyor of war propaganda has been expanded by the author in a 2004 edition entitled *The First Casualty: The War Correspondent as Hero and Myth-Maker from the Crimea to Iraq* (ISBN 0801880300).

evidence. The Right Sector leader Dmytro Yarosh hailed the massacre as 'another bright day in our national history.' In the American and British media, this was reported as a 'murky tragedy' resulting from 'clashes' between 'nationalists' (neo-Nazis) and 'separatists' (people collecting signatures for a referendum on a federal Ukraine). The *New York Times* buried it, having dismissed as Russian propaganda warnings about the fascist and anti-Semitic policies of Washington's new clients. The *Wall Street Journal* damned the victims — 'Deadly Ukraine Fire Likely Sparked by Rebels, Government Says.' Obama congratulated the junta for its 'restraint.'

"On 28 June, the *Guardian* devoted most of a page to declarations by the Kiev regime's 'president,' the oligarch Petro Poroshenko. Again, Orwell's rule of inversion applied. There was no putsch; no war against Ukraine's minority; the Russians were to blame for everything. 'We want to modernize my country,' said Poroshenko. 'We want to introduce freedom, democracy, and European values. Somebody doesn't like that. Somebody doesn't like us for that.'

"According to his report, the *Guardian*'s reporter, Luke Harding, did not challenge these assertions, or mention the Odessa atrocity, the regime's air and artillery attacks on residential areas, the killing and kidnapping of journalists, the firebombing of an opposition newspaper and his threat to 'free Ukraine from dirt and parasites.' The enemy are 'rebels,' 'militants,' 'insurgents,' 'terrorists' and stooges of the Kremlin.

"The current campaign to blame the Russian government for the downing of the Malaysian airliner is part of this propaganda. In truth, the crime of the airliner's shooting down is a direct result of Obama's putsch in Ukraine. Summon from history the ghosts of Vietnam, Chile, East Timor, southern Africa, Iraq; note the same propagated tags, the same false flags. Palestine is the lodestone of this unchanging deceit. Following the latest Israeli, American-equipped slaughter in Gaza of more than 800 Palestinians — including 120 children — an Israeli general writes in the *Guardian* under the headline, 'A necessary show of force.'"[103]

[103]   John Pilger, "The Return of George Orwell and Big Brother's war on Palestine, Ukraine and the Truth," johnpilger.com: The Films and Journalism of John Pilger, July 11, 2014; http://johnpilger.com/articles/the-return-of-george-orwell-and-big-brothers-war-on-palestine-ukraine-and-truth

The United States conducted a secret atomic and nuclear weapons testing program in the Pikinni atoll of the Marshall Islands between 1946 and 1958. (Pictured here is the blast from "Romeo" of Operation Castle in 1954.) Native residents agreed to leave Pikinni island on the assurance of the U.S. military that they would shortly be able to return to their homes after the tests, which the government was conducting for "the good of mankind and to end all world wars."

Early testing involved atomic bombs, and proceeded as expected. Then in 1954, Operation Castle introduced testing of the newly designed thermonuclear hydrogen bomb. The first of these tests, at dawn on March 1st, produced an explosion that far exceeded the predictions of scientists and military authorities. The new weapon proved to be about 1000 times more powerful and destructive than the atomic bombs used in World War II, and it destroyed many of the instruments intended to measure its blast.

The blast produced widespread nuclear contamination, with radioactive fallout reaching Australia, India, and Japan, and even as far as the United States and parts of Europe.

More immediately, the U.S. firing crew that detonated the device from Enyu island had to be evacuated in an airlift rescue operation. About two hours after the blast, radioactive fallout began to rain down on a Japanese fishing boat eighty miles downwind of the Pikinni atoll, causing acute radiation poisoning in all 23 crew members, and eventually killing 12 of them.

The Rongelap and Rongerik atolls were evacuated within 48 hours of the blast, and the more distant Utrik atoll within 72 hours, but not soon enough to prevent the inhabitants from experiencing severe radiation effects.

In 1972, about 100 members of the displaced islanders attempted to return to their home, but they were evacuated again ten years later when the locally grown food was determined to be causing cancer, miscarriages, still-births, and genetic birth defects.

In the end, the United States government paid $150 million in compensation to the natives of Pikinni Island and to their descendants for damages and displacement from their homeland. Three islands of the atoll had been vaporized in the course of the testing, and a 1998 report by the International Atomic Energy Agency concluded that the island remains unsafe for resettlement.

CHAPTER 4
What Will Nuclear War Be Like?

The whole scheme of making a "successful" nuclear first strike against a nation is not only murderous, but suicidal. Even if the U.S. did manage to destroy Russia (or *vice versa*, if Russia were to destroy the U.S.) in a nuclear assault in such a way as to eliminate the other country's ability to launch any retaliatory weapons of its own, the resulting fires would send so much soot into the atmosphere that the whole world would be plunged into a "nuclear winter" for years to come. Agricultural production would collapse, and even those people who did not die of the blast or from the spreading radiation effects would die of starvation.

Steven Starr of Physicians for Social Responsibility[104] addressed the U.N. General Assembly in 2011, describing the inevitable and catastrophic environmental consequences of any nuclear war — even a small-scale exchange in a regional war, such as between India and Pakistan. Every nation, he argued, has an urgent reason to rethink their notions of modern warfare. A nuclear strike launched by any nation will bring a suicidal *self-assured destruction even to that nation*:

> "[T]he detonation of even a tiny fraction of the global nuclear arsenal in urban areas will cause catastrophic damage to the Earth's climate and environment. ... [T]he environmental consequences of a "regional" nuclear war, fought between India and Pakistan, would cause a global famine....

> "[T]he detonation of 100 [comparatively small] 15-kiloton nuclear weapons in Indian and Pakistani megacities would create urban firestorms that would loft 5 million tons of thick, black, radioactive smoke above cloud level. This smoke would engulf the entire planet within 10 days. Because the smoke couldn't be rained out, it would remain in the stratosphere for at least a decade, and would heat the upper atmosphere, ...caus[ing] massive destruction of the protective stratospheric ozone, while simultaneously blocking warming sunlight, and creating Ice Age weather conditions on Earth. Average surface temperatures would become colder than any experienced in the last 1000 years.

> "Humans have had some experience with this sort of deadly global climate change. In 1815, the largest volcanic eruption in recorded history took place in Indonesia. Mount Tambora exploded and created a stratospheric layer of sulfuric acid droplets that blocked sunlight from reaching Earth. During the following year, which became known as "the year without a

---

[104] See the website at www.psr.org See also his own website at www.nucleardarkness.org. He has also published on the Moscow Institute of Physics and Technology's website for Strategic Arms Reduction (STAR), and in the online magazine "Bulletin of the Atomic Scientists" (http://thebulletin.org/).

summer," the northeastern United States experienced snowstorms in June and killing frosts every month of the year. At the same time, there was famine in Europe. …

"Ten years after a regional nuclear war, Earth's average surface temperatures would still be as cold, or colder, than they were in 1816. Most likely, the long-lived smoke layer would produce a 'decade without a summer.'"[105]

What about a nuclear war between major world powers such as the U.S., Russia, and China? Very simple. As Starr explains,

"Nuclear war has no winner. … [A] war fought with less than half of US or Russian strategic nuclear weapons would destroy the human race. … A war fought with [all of] the deployed U.S. and Russian nuclear arsenals would leave the Earth virtually uninhabitable."[106]

The fires caused by even a "restrained" nuclear exchange between the U.S. and Russia would leave the earth exposed to deadly levels of UV radiation passing through an ozone-depleted atmosphere. Temperatures throughout the central U.S. and Eurasia would fall below freezing after sunfall every day for up to three years, completely eliminating growing seasons. Starr's United Nations speech continues:

"[E]ven a 'successful' first strike by Washington or Moscow, which completely destroyed the opposing side's nuclear forces, would inflict catastrophic environmental damage that would make agriculture impossible and cause global famine. The detonation of the 2000 strategic weapons the US and Russia now have on high-alert would … constitute a self-destruct mechanism for humanity."

Firestorms

The horrific urban fires caused by nuclear warheads are difficult to imagine. When Chicago burned in October 1871, the fire (which started in the O'Leary barn when a cow kicked over a lantern) spread from house to house over a period of about two days until much of the city was in ruins. San Francisco, with its closely packed wooden homes and buildings, has unfortunately suffered similar fires many times.

These are examples of *line-fires, which spread along the burning periphery of a smoldering interior region*. By comparison these are rather tame events, usually causing small loss of life, and quite limited in the amount of heat and smoke produced.

The 1906 San Francisco earthquake, however, produced a categorically different

[105] Steven Starr, Address to the United Nations General Assembly; http://www.wagingpeace.org/wp-content/uploads/2012/11/2010_10_25_starr_1stcomm.pdf

[106] Steven Starr, *ibid.*, and "There Can be No Winners in a Nuclear War"; http://www.truth-out.org/speakout/item/24290-there-can-be-no-winners-in-a-nuclear-war

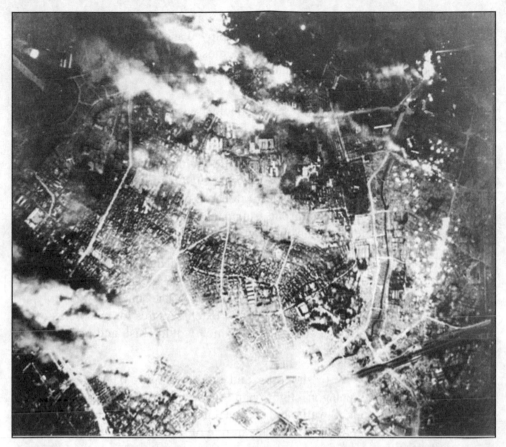

Hell on earth — a human furnace. In the firebombing of Tokyo on the night of March 9-10, 1945, under General LeMay's direction, two hundred and seventy-nine B-29 bombers dropped 1700 tons of self-scattering incendiary materials over the city, producing a single enormous inferno.

phenomenon. Ruptured gas lines throughout the city caused fires to break out simultaneously over a large area, which (since the water mains were also broken) quickly became a single enormous fire.

The same effect was produced intentionally with incendiary bombs in Hamburg, Dresden, and Tokyo during World War II, with tens of thousands of casualties in each case. Such a large fire, when virtually a whole city is burning at once, produces a *firestorm* — a super-heated storm-force wind system, drawing in air from all sides at hurricane speed, which stokes the fire up to an even greater intensity, making it in effect a blast furnace.

Sadly, the horrific fires produced by even the worst of the tragic bombings of the Second World War (including the atomic bombing of Hiroshima) were mere shadows of what a *nuclear firestorm* would be like. Each of today's *strategic nuclear* weapons (as opposed to the miniature "tactical" nuclear weapons used on battlefields, or the first-generation "atomic" bombs used on Nagasaki and Hiroshima) could easily ignite

63

a firestorm covering more than 100 square miles — and the U.S. and Russia each have thousands of these strategic nuclear weapons deployed and ready for immediate use.

The destructive power of these weapons almost defies imagination. Steven Starr explains in detail some of the devastation that would be experienced after a nuclear blast above Washington, D.C.:

"[A] single average sized strategic nuclear weapon … has an explosive power of 300 kilotons (kT), equaling 600 million pounds of dynamite…. [If such a weapon were] detonated at an altitude of 1500 feet above the Pentagon in Washington, D.C., … [it] would within a millionth of a second release 300 trillion calories of energy primarily in the form of intense light. The surrounding air would be superheated and create a rapidly expanding fireball. Almost all the air within and around the fireball would be compressed into a steeply fronted luminous blast wave of enormous extent and power.

"The fireball would extend more than a mile in diameter and at its center produce temperatures of over 200 million degrees Fahrenheit, about four to five times the temperature found at the center of the sun. This unearthly release of heat and energy would … ignite extensive fires for many tens of square miles and produce a blast wave which would crush and tear apart any structures in its path. …

"At Pentagon City (a shopping and office complex 0.7 miles from ground zero at the Pentagon), light from the fireball would melt asphalt in the streets, burn paint off walls, and melt metal surfaces within a half second of detonation. The interior of vehicles in line of sight of the fireball would explode into flames.

"About one second later, the blast wave and 750-mph winds would arrive and toss burning and disintegrating vehicles into the air like leaves in a wind. The blast wave could cave in buildings and would turn windows and furniture into missiles and shrapnel. The interiors of buildings that remained standing would, within minutes, be burning pyres of splintered walls, doors and other combustibles. Seconds after the passage of the blast wave, suction effects created in part by the rising fireball would reverse the winds, drawing them toward the detonation point at perhaps 50 – 70 mph. …

"Grass, vegetation, and leaves on trees would explode into flames, and the surface of the ground would explode into superheated dust. Flames and black smoke would spew out from all combustible materials illuminated by the fireball. … Birds in flight would drop from the sky in flames. People exposed to the light would be instantly cremated.

"Four seconds later the blast wave would arrive and collapse the

64

Jefferson and Lincoln memorials. This would be followed by winds of 300-400 mph which combining with the blast wave would completely destroy wood-frame and residential brick buildings. ...

"Within 3 miles of ground zero the clothing worn by people in direct line of sight of the fireball would burst into flames or melt, and areas of skin not covered by clothing would be scorched, charring flesh and causing third-degree burns. ...

[T]here would be a mass fire ignited to a distance of just over 4.5 miles from the detonation. This gigantic fire would quickly increase in intensity and in minutes generate ground winds of hurricane force with average air temperatures well above the boiling point of water.... Those who sought to flee through the streets would be burned alive by hurricane-force winds laden with flames and firebrands. ... There would be no escape. The fire would eliminate all life in the fire zone."The smoke and mushroom cloud, seething with radioactivity, would rise up to blot out the sun. Deadly fallout would contaminate hundreds of square miles downwind with radioactive poisons from the blast, dooming hundreds of thousands of humans and animals to a painful, vicious death from radiation sickness. Much of the land contaminated by the fallout would remain uninhabitable for years."

Starr concludes his description with this sobering note:

"If you live in a large city in the U.S. or Russia, or in any other nation possessing nuclear weapons, there is at least one nuclear warhead aimed at you. ... Imagine this same event happening, in less than an hour, with not one, but with thousands of strategic nuclear weapons detonating in the cities of the U.S., Russia, China, Europe, India, and Pakistan."[107]

Meltdown

Besides the catastrophic environmental effects of the millions of tons of smoke that would be produced in a nuclear war, there is another major concern. The electro-magnetic pulse (EMP) generated by an atmospheric nuclear explosion would destroy the electronic cooling systems of nuclear power plants within the target radius, immediately causing meltdown disasters.

A single large nuclear warhead detonated at an altitude of 300 miles above the central region of the United States would destroy electronic systems throughout the entire continental U.S., causing simultaneous meltdowns at nuclear power plants across the country. A lower-altitude blast would have a smaller radius of direct damage from its electro-magnetic pulse, but electrical power would likely be lost even outside of the

---

[107]   Steven Starr, "The Effects of a 300 Kiloton Nuclear Warhead Detonated above Washington, D.C."; http://www.wagingpeace.org/author/steven-starr/

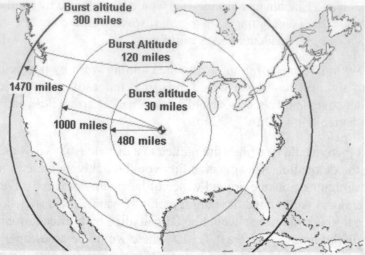

EMP AREA BY BURSTS AT 30, 120 and 300 MILES
Gary Smith, "Electromagnetic Pulse Threats", testimony to House
National Security Committee on July 16, 1997

The electromagnetic pulse generated by a single nuclear warhead detonated 300 miles above the earth's surface could affect the entire continental United States.

target radius due to the damage to the nation's power grid. Nuclear power plants outside of the EMP radius could therefore prevent meltdowns only as long as their diesel-fueled generators could be kept running. When the fuel runs out, Fukushima-type disasters[108] would occur all across the land. Steven Starr explains:

> "Electromagnetic pulse from high-altitude nuclear detonations would destroy the integrated circuits in all modern electronic devices, including those in commercial nuclear power plants. Every nuclear reactor would almost instantly meltdown; every nuclear spent fuel pool (which contain many times more radioactivity than found in the reactors) would boil off, releasing vast amounts of long-lived radioactivity. The fallout would make most of the US and Europe uninhabitable."[109]

But our problems would not end there. American and European society depends today to a large extent on electricity for food production and distribution, as well as for medical care, law enforcement, banking, communication, etc. Our standard of living

---

[108]   For an assessment of how much biological and environmental damage the Fukushima accident has already caused, see Susie Greaves, "Tokyo Contaminated & Not Fit for Habitation, Doctor Says," The Permaculture Research Institute, September 25, 2014 (http://permaculturenews.org/2014/09/25/tokyo-contaminated-fit-habitation-doctor-says/); Dr. Mae-Wan Ho, "Truth about Fukushima," Institute of Science in Society, May 6, 2012, (http://www.i-sis.org.uk/Truth_About_Fukushima.php); and Dr. Mae-Wan Ho, "Fukushima Crisis Goes Global," The Permaculture Research Institute, January 8, 2014 (http://permaculturenews.org/2014/01/08/fukushima-crisis-goes-global/).

[109]   Steven Starr, "There Can be No Winners in a Nuclear War"; http://www.truth-out.org/speakout/item/24290-there-can-be-no-winners-in-a-nuclear-war

Nuclear power reactors are distributed throughout the U.S. and Europe. The burst of electromagnetic radiation emanating from a high-altitude nuclear explosion could turn each one into a Fukushima-type disaster site, making these entire regions of the world uninhabitable.

may seem an improvement over the conditions in which our grandparents lived, but in fact we are now critically vulnerable to privation, disease, and lawlessness, such as they never experienced. While previous generations from the time of Adam were able to live with reasonable comfort without electricity, it is now estimated that within twelve months of a nationwide blackout, up to 90% of the U.S. population might perish in the ensuing societal breakdown. Professor William Forstchen explains:

"[W]herever [an electromagnetic pulse] strikes wires, metal surfaces, antennas, or power lines, it will travel along those metal surfaces…. The longer the wire, the more energy is absorbed. A miles-long high-tension wire will absorb tens of thousands of amps, and here is where the destruction begins, as [the current] slams into any delicate electronic circuits…. In far less than a millisecond, the entire power grid of the United States…will be destroyed. …

"[B]etween 250,000 to 500,000 people will die in the first few minutes…. All [planes in flight] would be doomed, the pilots sitting impotent, staring

67

at blank computer screens, pulling on controls that no longer respond as the plane finally noses over and heads in. …

"[H]ospitals and nursing homes…have back-up generators, but those generators are "hot-wired" into the building so power can instantly kick in if the main system shuts down. That "hot wiring" means the Electro Magnetic Pulse will take out the generators and their circuitry as well. …

"Nearly everyone dependent on life support equipment in ICUs will be dead within hours. Nearly everyone in nursing homes dependent on oxygen generators, respirators, etc., will be dead or dying. And depending on the time of year, temperatures within buildings will plummet or soar. …

"Twelve hours later the food in your freezer starts to thaw. If it is winter and you don't have a wood stove, the frost will start to penetrate into your house….

"Food that starts to thaw, which we were always cautioned to throw out, or food in a refrigerator that is now at room temperature — do you throw it out or risk eating it? If your house is fully electric, how do you cook it properly?

"These few questions alone [point to] an entire nation heading into gastro-intestinal aliments within a week to ten days…. Very young children and the elderly can die in less than a day from severe dehydration and electrolyte imbalance. Without plenty of clean water and modern waste removal, the problem gets far worse…. Where do they get safe water? The nearby stream or river is now a dump for raw sewage since purification plants are off line. … [Soon] more serious diseases will appear — pneumonia (especially in the winter due to exposure), more exotic and dangerous types of food-poisoning such as salmonella due to a complete collapse of sanitation, various forms of hepatitis, even diseases scarcely heard of in a generation or more — measles, scarlet fever, and tuberculosis. …

"Those who are dependent on medications to control asthma, heart disease, diabetes, and a host of other aliments [will die] within days or weeks….

"Our interstate highways will become nightmare paths of exile as our largely urban population tries to fan out to find food that once was shipped in. Millions will die on that road.

"And finally, violence, … [as people] begin to kill each other for food, water, and shelter. … After sixty days, starvation will be killing off millions, and by 120 days, mass starvation will be the norm. ... [It] could very well be that in a year's time, nine out of ten Americans will be dead."[110]

Human Delusions

Finally, Starr comments on the gravity of the human element of the nuclear threat:

"Theories of 'limited nuclear war' and 'nuclear de-escalation' are unrealistic. Once nuclear weapons were introduced into a US-Russian conflict, there would be little chance that a nuclear holocaust could be avoided. ...

"Counterforce doctrine — used by both the US and Russian military — emphasizes the need for preemptive strikes once nuclear war begins. Both sides would be under immense pressure to launch a preemptive nuclear first strike once military hostilities had commenced, especially if [tactical] nuclear weapons had already been used on the battlefield.

"Both the US and Russia each have 400 to 500 launch-ready ballistic missiles armed with a total of at least 1800 strategic nuclear warheads, which can be launched with only a few minutes warning. Both the US and Russian Presidents are accompanied 24/7 [24 hours per day, 7 days per week] by military officers carrying a 'nuclear briefcase,' which allows them to transmit the permission order to launch in a matter of seconds.

"Yet top political leaders and policymakers of both the US and Russia seem to be unaware that their launch-ready nuclear weapons represent a self-destruct mechanism for the human race. ... [E]ven a 'successful' nuclear first strike, which destroyed 100% of the opposing side's nuclear weapons, would cause the citizens of the side that 'won' the nuclear war to perish from nuclear famine, just as would the rest of humanity. ...

"Even more frightening is the fact that the [officials] running US foreign policy believe that the US has 'nuclear primacy' over Russia; that is, [that] the US could successfully launch a nuclear sneak-attack against Russian (and Chinese) nuclear forces and completely destroy them. This theory was articulated in 2006 in 'The Rise of U.S. Nuclear Primacy,'[111] which was published in *Foreign Affairs* by the Council on Foreign Relations. By concluding that the Russians and Chinese would be unable to retaliate, or if some small part of their forces remained, would not risk a second US attack

---

[110]   William R. Forstchen, Ph.D., "EMP 101: A Basic Primer"; http://www.onesecondafter.com/pb/wp_d10e87d9/wp_d10e87d9.html

[111]   Keir A. Lieber and Daryl G. Press, "The Rise of U.S. Nuclear Primacy," April 2006, *Foreign Affairs*; http://www.foreignaffairs.com/articles/61508/keir-a-lieber-and-daryl-g-press/the-rise-of-us-nuclear-primacy

by retaliating, the article invites nuclear war."[112]

The devil will be the only winner in a nuclear confrontation between nations of virtually any size, since the vast majority of people throughout the world will die. Paul Craig Roberts puts it in a nutshell:

"As neither side can afford to lose the [coming] war, the war would be nuclear. As scientists have made clear, life on earth would cease, regardless of whether Washington's ABM shield works. This is why I oppose Washington's policies and speak out against the arrogance and hubris that define Washington today. The most likely outcome of Washington's pursuit of world hegemony is the extinction of life on earth."[113]

Why This Madness?

Our situation is dire, and almost defies understanding. John Pilger marvels at the West's provocations toward Russia, threatening all of humanity:

"Since the collapse of the Soviet Union, the United States has ringed Russia with military bases, nuclear warplanes, and missiles as part of its 'NATO Enlargement Project.' Reneging on a promise made to Soviet President Mikhail Gorbachev in 1990 that NATO would not expand 'one inch to the east,' NATO has, in effect, militarily occupied Eastern Europe. In the former Soviet Caucasus, NATO's expansion is the biggest military build-up since the Second World War.

"A NATO Membership Action Plan is Washington's gift to the coup-regime in Kiev. In August, 'Operation Rapid Trident' [put] American and British troops on Ukraine's Russian border, and 'Sea Breeze' [sent] US warships within sight of Russian ports. Imagine the response if these acts of provocation, or intimidation, were carried out on America's borders. …

"Confounding the war parties in Washington and Kiev, Vladimir Putin withdrew troops from the Ukrainian border and urged ethnic Russians in eastern Ukraine to abandon separatism. In Orwellian fashion, this has been inverted in the West to the 'Russian threat.'

"Hillary Clinton likened Putin to Hitler. Without irony, right-wing German commentators said as much. In the media, the Ukrainian neo-Nazis are sanitized as 'nationalists' or 'ultra-nationalists.' What they fear is that Putin is skillfully seeking a diplomatic solution, and may succeed.

---

[112] Steven Starr, "There Can be No Winners in a Nuclear War"; http://www.truth-out.org/speakout/item/24290-there-can-be-no-winners-in-a-nuclear-war

[113] Paul Craig Roberts, "Can Putin's Diplomacy Prevail Over Washington's Coercion?" June 24, 2014; http://www.paulcraigroberts.org/2014/06/24/can-putins-diplomacy-prevail-washingtons-coercion-paul-craig-roberts/

"On 27 June, responding to Putin's latest accommodation (his request to the Russian Parliament to rescind legislation that gave him the power to intervene on behalf of Ukraine's ethnic Russians), Secretary of State John Kerry issued another of his ultimatums. Russia must 'act within the next few hours, literally' to end the revolt in eastern Ukraine.

"Notwithstanding that Kerry is widely recognized as a buffoon, the serious purpose of these 'warnings' is to confer pariah status on Russia...."[114]

In another place, Pilger draws back the curtain for us on the larger context of this U.S. expansionist drive. Commenting on the Obama administration's China containment policy[115] (according to which the U.S. would attempt to surround China with naval and air bases, and to interject itself into China's disputes with its Asian neighbors), he demonstrates an even bleaker picture than the single threat of war developing between the West and Russia:

"On 24 April, President Obama [began] a tour of Asia to promote his 'Pivot to China.' The aim [was] to convince his 'allies' in the region, principally Japan, to re-arm and prepare for the eventual possibility of war with China. By 2020, almost two-thirds of all US naval forces in the world will be transferred to the Asia-Pacific area. This is the greatest military concentration in that vast region since the Second World War.

"In an arc extending from Australia to Japan, China will face US missiles and nuclear-armed bombers. A strategic naval base is being built on the Korean island of Jeju less than 400 miles from the Chinese metropolis of Shanghai and the industrial heartland of the only country whose economic power is likely to surpass that of the US. Obama's 'pivot' is designed to undermine China's influence in its region. It is as if world war has begun by other means. ...

"Obama's Defense Secretary, Charles 'Chuck' Hagel, was in Beijing last week to deliver a menacing warning that China, like Russia, could face isolation and war if it did not bow to US demands. He compared the annexation of Crimea with China's complex territorial dispute with Japan over uninhabited islands in the East China Sea. 'You cannot go around the world,' said Hagel with a straight face, 'and violate the sovereignty of nations by force, coercion, or intimidation.' As for America's massive

114   John Pilger, "The Return of George Orwell and Big Brother's War on Palestine, Ukraine and the Truth," johnpilger.com: The Films and Journalism of John Pilger, July 11, 2014; http://johnpilger.com/articles/the-return-of-george-orwell-and-big-brothers-war-on-palestine-ukraine-and-truth

115   The "Pivot to Asia" was first announced by then Secretary of State Hillary Clinton in 2011. Cf. Hillary Rodham Clinton, "America's Pacific Century," U.S. Department of State, via Foreign Policy Magazine, October 11, 2011; http://iipdigital.usembassy.gov/st/english/article/2011/10/20111011161233su0.8861287.html#axzz30Ph1DmRw

movement of naval forces and nuclear weapons to Asia, that is 'a sign of the humanitarian assistance the US military can provide.'

"Obama is currently seeking a greater budget for nuclear weapons than the historical peak during the Cold War…. The United States is pursuing its longstanding ambition to dominate the Eurasian landmass, stretching from China to Europe: a 'manifest destiny' made right by might."[116]

It is clear that a major and terrible war is coming soon. Western leaders are rattling their sabers, stirring up a "war fever" through the slavishly compliant mainstream media. These same leaders are using the media to demonize and isolate foes, and are antagonizing Russia with economic sanctions and with war games and other war preparations along Russia's borders. Heinous crimes are committed, apparently in order to fuel more war propaganda, to increase tensions and to justify greater military mobilization.

Actions have already begun to follow — and will continue to follow — this war rhetoric and these provocations, just as surely as the purpose of rhetoric is to pave the way for action.

Gabor Steingart points out that even at the height of the Cold War, when Russia built the Berlin Wall, West Germany did not resort to using war rhetoric against East Germany. Steingart highly praises Willy Brandt, at that time the Mayor of Berlin, for this level-headed restraint:

"Just consider what Willy Brandt had to listen to when his fate as mayor of Berlin placed him in the shadow of the wall. What sanctions and punishments were suggested to him. But he decided to forgo this festival of outrage. He never turned the screw of retribution. …

"Willy Brandt decided clearly differently than Merkel in the present, and that in a clearly more intense situation. As he recalls, he had awoken on the morning of August 13, 1961 'wide awake and at the same time numb,' … when he received reports from Berlin about work being done on the large wall separating the city. It was a Sunday morning and the humiliation could hardly be greater for a sitting mayor.

"The Soviets had presented him with a *fait accompli*. … Brandt remembers that an 'impotent rage' had risen in him. But what did he do? He reined in his feelings of impotence and displayed his great talent as reality-based politician which would garner him a stint as Chancellor and finally also the Nobel Prize for Peace. …

"[H]e accepted the new situation, knowing that no amount of outrage

116   John Pilger, "The Strangelove Effect – Or How We Are Hoodwinked into Accepting a New World War," johnpilger.com: The Films and Journalism of John Pilger, April 18, 2014; http://johnpilger.com/articles/the-strangelove-effect-or-how-we-are-hoodwinked-into-accepting-a-new-world-war

from the rest of the world would bring this wall down again for a while. He even ordered the West Berlin police to use batons and water cannons against demonstrators at the wall in order not to slip from the catastrophe of division into the much greater catastrophe of war. He strove for the paradox which Bahr put as follows later: 'We acknowledged the Status Quo in order to change it.' …

"And they managed to accomplish this change. Brandt and Bahr made the specific interests of the West Berlin population for whom they were now responsible … into the measure of their politics. … They negotiated a travel permit treaty with East Berlin which made the wall permeable again two years after it was put up. Between Christmas 1963 and New Year's 1964, 700,000 inhabitants of Berlin visited their relatives in the east of the city. Every tear of joy turned into a vote for Brandt a short while later.

"The voters realized that here was someone who wanted to affect the way they lived every day, not just generate a headline for the next morning. In an almost completely hopeless situation, this SPD man fought for western values — in this case the values of freedom of movement — without bullhorns, without sanctions, without the threat of violence."[117]

If we can keep a level-headed perspective, we will realize that the burden of proof rests on the accuser. It is never enough for someone to simply say, "Get angry with this person because I say so!" In the present instance, it would be difficult to maintain that Western leaders and the mainstream media have given us sufficient and credible evidence to support the claim that the separatists in Ukraine are the murders of the unfortunate victims on MH-17.

If, on the other hand, (as a substantial body of evidence seems to suggest) Ukraine was responsible for shooting down the Malaysia Airlines plane, it would follow that the United States was also involved. As Russian Foreign Minister Sergei Lavrov has remarked,[118] the U.S. has been "running the show" in Ukraine all along, ever since the February uprisings that led to the ousting of President Yanukovych.

But then if it was Washington that was ultimately behind the destruction of MH-17, how can we explain President Obama's seemingly reckless and relentless provocations toward Russia over Ukraine?

Stephen Lendman, co-author of the book *Flashpoint in Ukraine: U.S. Drive for Hegemony Risks WW III*, describes Ukraine as "the crown jewel" in Washington's quest for "unchallenged global dominance" over the former Warsaw Pact nations:

"Washington wants all of these countries turning west and incorporated

---

[117]   *Loc. cit.*

[118]   *Cf.* Sophie Shevardnadze, "Lavrov to RT: Americans Are 'Running the Show' in Ukraine," April 23, 2014, *RT*; http://rt.com/shows/sophieco/154364-lavrov-ukraine-standoff-sophieco/

73

into NATO, with U.S. bases bordering Russia and nuclear missiles targeting its heartland. It wants Russia systematically marginalized, weakened, isolated and co-opted as just another subservient Western vassal state."[119]

Lendman's assessment seems to correspond to how the tragedy of MH-17 has been used by Western governments — to justify more sanctions against Russia, as well as more military aid for the new regime in Kiev and more military build-up along Russia's borders.

But regardless of our leaders' reasons for their actions, when the next war comes it will be at a terrible price for us all.

[119] Interview with Keith Johnson, "What's Really Going on in Ukraine?" May 26, 2014, *American Free Press*, Issue 21, p. 18.

Part II:
The One and Only Solution

O MARY
CONCEIVED
WITHOUT SIN
PRAY FOR US
WHO HAVE
RECOURSE
TO THEE

HEART OF IMMACULATE MARY, PRAY FOR US.

As Our Lady of Fatima explained to the children seers, "God wills to establish in the world the devotion to My Immaculate Heart." When the Pope and, at his order, all the Catholic bishops of the world solemnly consecrate Russia to the Immaculate Heart of Mary, Our Lady's incomparable merits will earn for the world two tremendous, historic graces: conversion and peace. When Sister Lucy asked Our Lord why He would not grant these graces to the world without the Consecration of Russia, He answered: "Because I want My whole Church to acknowledge that Consecration as a Triumph of the Immaculate Heart of Mary so that it may extend Its cult later on and place the devotion to this Immaculate Heart beside the devotion to My Sacred Heart."

Chapter 1 • *In Essence*

It almost defies comprehension that any political leaders could be nonchalant about the risk of taking their country into war — or worse, that anyone could desire to bring on a war — but in fact, war is at the heart of the program planned by secret societies to remake the world according to a New World Order. The wars of the past century in particular have enabled Freemasonry to accomplish their goals very rapidly, to overthrow the remnants of the Christian social order and to set up new (godless) programs and institutions throughout much of the world.

The hellish nightmare of a World War has already twice been purposely inflicted on mankind,[120] and a third such war now faces us as an imminent threat. Heaven has provided us with a solution to this threat, but at the same time, God has laid down the conditions of that one and only solution:

- **God will grant this grace of world peace through the Immaculate Heart of Mary** — Peace in the whole world will come through the intervention of the Immaculate Heart of Mary, and particularly through Her intervention on behalf of Russia. Our Lord has especially entrusted the salvation of Russia and the peace of the world to the Immaculate Heart of Mary, as He told Sister Lucy in a revelation of 1936, and as Our Lady of Fatima revealed to the children seers:

> "[Our Lord said to me,] 'The Immaculate Heart of Mary will save Russia. It has been entrusted to Her.'"[121]

> "A little while before going to hospital, Jacinta [one of the seers of Fatima] said to me: 'Tell everybody that God grants us graces through the Immaculate Heart of Mary; that people are to ask Her for them; and that the Heart of Jesus wants the Immaculate Heart of Mary to be venerated at His side. Tell them also to pray to the Immaculate Heart of

---

[120] Both Karl Marx and Friedrich Engels (co-authors of the *Communist Manifesto*) wrote explicitly in 1848 about instigating a world war in order to further the "progress" of history toward the goals of Communism, and Albert Pike (author of *Morals and Dogma of the Ancient and Accepted Scottish Rite*) predicted in 1871 that three world wars would be needed to completely dissolve all national sovereignties into a global collectivist state. (See Choosing Truth Ministries, *Freemasonry On Trial*, 2003 edition, Part Two, pp. 22-23; http://www.pdfarchive.info/pdf/F/Fr/Freemasonry_on_trial.pdf) For a detailed discussion of international bankers' role in the orchestration and deliberate instigation of World War II, see Chapter 9 of Deirdre Manifold, *Towards World Government*, Canisius Books, Toronto, 2nd edition, 1993.

[121] Sister Lucy's letter of May 18, 1936 to Father José Gonçalves, cited in Frère Michel de la Sainte Trinité, *The Whole Truth About Fatima*, Volume II, Immaculate Heart Publications, Buffalo, New York, 1989, p. 631.

Mary for peace, since God has entrusted it to Her.'"[122]

- **By Means of the Consecration of Russia** — By Our Lord's express command to His Church, this intervention is to be sought and obtained by a solemn and public ceremony of prayer and reparation, in which the Holy Father, in union with all the Catholic bishops of the world, consecrates specifically Russia to the Immaculate Heart of Mary, as was revealed to Sister Lucy in 1929:

> "Our Lady said, 'The moment has come in which God asks of the Holy Father to make, and to order that in union with him and at the same time, all the bishops of the world make the consecration of Russia to My Immaculate Heart,' promising to convert it because of this day of prayer and world-wide reparation."[123]

- **By no other means than the Consecration of Russia** — There is absolutely no other possibility for avoiding the coming wars than obeying Heaven's command for the Consecration of Russia, as Our Lord told Sister Lucy in 1936, and as Our Lady emphasized again to her in 1952:

> "Intimately I have spoken to Our Lord about the subject, and not too long ago I asked Him *why He would not convert Russia without the Holy Father making that consecration?* 'Because I want My whole Church to acknowledge that Consecration as a Triumph of the Immaculate Heart of Mary, so that it may extend Its cult later on, and place the devotion to this Immaculate Heart beside the devotion to My Sacred Heart.'"[124]

> "Make it known to the Holy Father that I still await the consecration of Russia to My Immaculate Heart. *Without this consecration Russia cannot be converted, nor can the world have peace.*"[125]

Moreover, we know without any doubt that in the end (possibly after great trials for the world, including the annihilation of various nations), the Pope and the bishops will obey Heaven's command for the Consecration of Russia, and that the graces of conversion and world peace will follow, as Our Lady promised to the children seers in 1917, and as Our Lord confirmed to Sister Lucy in 1931 and again in 1936:

> "If My requests are heeded, Russia will be converted, and there will be peace; if not, she will spread her errors throughout the world, causing wars

---

122   Third Memoir; *Fatima in Lucia's Own Words*, English translation by Dominican Nuns of Perpetual Rosary, Fatima, Portugal, 1976, p. 116.

123   Manuscript from Sister Lucy's journal, cited in Frère Michel de la Sainte Trinité, *The Whole Truth About Fatima*, Volume II, Immaculate Heart Publications, Buffalo, New York, 1989, p. 555.

124   Sister Lucy's letter of May 18, 1936 to Father José Gonçalves, cited in Frère Michel de la Sainte Trinité, *The Whole Truth About Fatima*, Volume II, Immaculate Heart Publications, Buffalo, New York, 1989, p. 631. Emphasis added.

125   Reported in the Italian bishops' publication, *Il pellegrinaggio delle meraviglie*, 1960, p. 440. Cited in Frère Michel, *The Whole Truth About Fatima*, vol. III, p. 327. Emphasis added.

and persecutions of the Church. The good will be martyred, the Holy Father will have much to suffer, various nations will be annihilated. … In the end, My Immaculate Heart will triumph. The Holy Father will consecrate Russia to Me. Russia will be converted, and a period of peace will be given to the world."[126]

"[B]y means of an interior communication, Our Lord complainingly said to me: 'They did not want to heed My request. Like the King of France they will repent and do so, but it will be late. Russia will already have spread her errors throughout the world, causing wars and persecutions of the Church. The Holy Father will have much to suffer!'"[127]

"'But my God, the Holy Father probably won't believe me, unless You Yourself move him with a special inspiration.'

"'The Holy Father. Pray very much for the Holy Father. He will do it, but it will be late! Nevertheless the Immaculate Heart of Mary will save Russia.'"[128]

There is no contradiction in these revelations, which warn of possible disasters ahead (including even the annihilation of nations), while at the same time promising the final triumph of the Immaculate Heart. The question is purely one of timing: Our Lady's triumph is sure "in the end." Whether or not the world suffers another global war, further persecutions of the Church, and the annihilation of nations *en route* to Our Lady's triumph depends on how long the Pope and bishops continue to delay their obedience to Heaven's command for the Consecration of Russia.

If we do nothing, there is going to be a war and it is going to be nuclear. Do we want to stop the coming war and the annihilation of nations? There is one way, and one way only: the Consecration of Russia.

But we're not the Pope. What can we do?

We need to realize first of all that our united voices have a great deal of moral authority, even if not *de jure* authority, within the Church. As members of a parish, members of a community, Members of Parliament, etc., we can powerfully petition the Holy Father to do what he needs to do. The message needs to be loud and clear: "Holy Father, we're in danger! We want you to consecrate Russia!"

You can stop the Third World War by signing such a petition, along with a sufficient number of others. How many others? God knows, but at some point it will be enough to draw a response from the Vatican. Our Lord is expecting us to do at least this much.

---

[126]   Spoken by Our Lady on July 13, 1917, within the context of the Great Secret of Fatima.

[127]   Revelation of August 1931, recounted in a letter of May 18, 1936 from Sister Lucy to her spiritual director, Father José Gonçalves, cited in Frère Michel de la Sainte Trinité, *The Whole Truth About Fatima*, Volume II, Immaculate Heart Publications, Buffalo, New York, 1989, p. 544.

[128]   Sister Lucy's letter of May 18, 1936 to Father José Gonçalves, cited in Frère Michel de la Sainte Trinité, *The Whole Truth About Fatima*, Volume II, Immaculate Heart Publications, Buffalo, New York, 1989, p. 631.

On the night of June 13, 1929, Our Lady appeared to Sister Lucy in her convent chapel, announcing Heaven's command for the immediate Consecration of Russia to Her Immaculate Heart. This solemn message was sealed with an unprecedented manifestation of the Blessed Trinity, with the Three Persons appearing together with Our Lady above the altar forming, as it were, an icon of our Redemption. Sister Lucy recounted the vision and message for her confessor: "Our Lady said, 'The moment has come in which God asks of the Holy Father to make, and to order that in union with him and at the same time all the bishops of the world make, the consecration of Russia to My Immaculate Heart,' promising to convert it because of this day of prayer and world-wide reparation."

Chapter 2 • In Detail

For the past nearly 100 years, Russia has served Divine Providence as the scourge of God's justice, bringing God's punishments to a whole world of guilty nations — fomenting wars and persecutions of the Church, and spreading diabolic errors throughout the world. Until Russia is properly consecrated in the manner specified by Our Lady of Fatima, it will continue in this divinely appointed role, leading (if it is not stopped in time) to even more widespread martyrdom and apostasy, and to the annihilation of various nations.

Sister Lucy, in a 1957 interview with Father Augustin Fuentes (which turned out to be her last unrestricted opportunity to speak publicly about the Message of Fatima), explained that Russia was the "instrument of chastisement" chosen by God to punish the world for its sins:

> "Tell them, Father, that many times the Most Holy Virgin told my cousins Francisco and Jacinta, as well as myself, that many nations will disappear from the face of the earth. She said that Russia will be the instrument of chastisement chosen by Heaven to punish the whole world if we do not beforehand obtain the conversion of that poor nation."[129]

But the only way to obtain the conversion of that poor nation is by the Consecration of Russia, as explained above. Tragically, this question — of whether or not we will manage to obtain the conversion of Russia in time to prevent the annihilation of nations — grows more doubtful with each passing day.

Nevertheless, the fact of Our Lady's coming Triumph through the miraculous conversion of Russia remains assured. On July 13, 1917, Our Lady of Fatima described to the three children-seers the sure Triumph of Her Immaculate Heart:

> "In the end, My Immaculate Heart will triumph. The Holy Father will consecrate Russia to Me. Russia will be converted, and a period of peace will be given to the world."

In this prophecy, Our Lady refers to a clear sequence of events ushering in the Triumph of Her Immaculate Heart: first, a triumph over the heart of the Pope, who will at last obey Our Lady's command and perform the Consecration of Russia; next, a triumph over the Russian nation, which will be miraculously brought back to the True Faith and to full communion with Peter's successor, the Pope; and finally, a triumph extending over mankind in general, in a worldwide period of peace, shattering for a long period of time the work and power of the devil in this world.

Father Nicholas Gruner of The Fatima Center (the largest apostolate in the world dedicated to promoting the Message of Fatima, and perhaps the only apostolate in the world which dares to do so in a manner completely faithful to Our Lady's Message) explains:

---

[129]   Cited in Frère Michel de la Sainte Trinité, *The Whole Truth About Fatima*, Volume III, Immaculate Heart Publications, Buffalo, New York, p. 505.

"Our Lady's triumph will be in three stages. The first stage is: 'The Holy Father will consecrate Russia to Me.' We have been waiting for the fulfillment of this stage for [now more than] ninety years.

"When Russia is at last consecrated, it will be converted. That is the second stage, which will take place within a couple of years of the Consecration.

"In the third stage, shortly after Russia is converted, peace will be given to the world. In the prophetic visions of St. John Bosco, we see that Russia will already have invaded the West before the Pope consecrates Russia. St. John Bosco had a vision of Russian armies in France carrying a black standard or flag, but while they are in France, he saw that their standard will turn from black to white. That will be when Russia has been consecrated, and it has converted. The Russian armies then will stay in France and Western Europe, not as enemies but as friends, to defend Europe from the invasion from the South. As St. John Bosco summarizes his dream, 'Salvation is from the North; danger is from the South' (meaning the Islamic armies that will march into Europe from the south). After their conversion, the Russians will remain in Western Europe and save it by defeating the Islamic armies. So the promise of peace is not instantaneous after the Consecration of Russia, but it will come shortly afterward."[130]

The Consecration of Russia —
Our Lady's Power Will Be Seen *"By This Means"*

What will be the significance of the Holy Father's consecration of Russia to Our Lady, making it so integral to Our Lady's Triumph? Let's look more closely at what Our Lady has said about this.

In the third of Our Lady's apparitions at Fatima, on July 13, 1917, the Blessed Virgin revealed to the three children a Great Secret, the first part of which was a momentary Vision of Hell. Immediately after that vision, Our Lady explained:

"You have seen hell where the souls of poor sinners go. To save them, God wills to establish in the world devotion to My Immaculate Heart. If what I say to you is done, many souls will be saved and there will be peace. … [God] is about to punish the world for its crimes, by means of war, famine, and persecutions of the Church and of the Holy Father. To prevent this, I shall come to ask for the consecration of Russia to My Immaculate Heart…."

Our Lady's words are very rich, and we cannot presume to unpack all of their

---

130 Father Nicholas Gruner, "Fatima and Our Lady's Immaculate Heart," *Fatima: Only Way to World Peace* Conference speech, August 20, 2007; http://www.fatimapeaceconferences.com/brazil_2007/transcripts/ fatima&olimh.pdf

meaning here. We could meditate on just these few words above, every day for many months, with great profit.

For the moment, let's take note of just these three key points:

1. Our Lady announced in 1917 that She would one day come again to ask for a particular act, the Consecration of Russia to Her Immaculate Heart. And why? In order to prevent the terrible punishments that would otherwise justly befall the world for its crimes.

2. In addition to preventing these punishments, there will follow an even greater effect of the Consecration, namely an unprecedented period of peace. The scourge of war, which has up until now plagued mankind virtually without interruption from the earliest times (14,400 wars in 6000 years of recorded history), will be halted all around the world.

3. The ultimate and greatest effect of this Consecration will be to establish in the world the devotion to the Immaculate Heart of Mary, thereby securing the salvation of many souls who would otherwise go to hell.

It was in 1929, twelve years after Our Lady's apparitions at Fatima, that Our Lady returned as She had promised to little 10-year-old Lucy (who was by this time a 22-year-old professed Sister in the Dorothean convent in Tuy, Spain). The date was June 13th.

Lucy was praying alone in the convent's chapel late that night, with her superiors' permission, making her routine Thursday night Holy Hour in honor of the Sacred Heart of Jesus (a devotion which Our Lord asked for through Saint Margaret Mary Alacoque).

Suddenly Our Lady of Fatima appeared on a little cloud above the altar, standing beside a great luminous Cross, on which Our Lord hung, crucified. Drops of Blood flowing from His Face and from the wound in His side fell upon a large Host suspended beneath His wounded side, and ran down across It into a chalice below.

God the Father and God the Holy Ghost manifested themselves visibly above Our Lord, absorbed in Their regard for His Sacrifice. And beneath the Cross, on the side opposite from Our Lady, were letters (as if of the clearest water, running down over the altar) forming the words: "Grace and Mercy." Our Lady held in Her left hand Her Immaculate Heart, circled with thorns, and in Her other hand a Rosary.

It will be worthwhile to read Sister Lucy's own account of this most extraordinary revelation:

"I had requested and obtained permission from my superiors and confessor to make the Holy Hour from 11:00 p.m. until midnight from Thursday to Friday.

"Being alone one night, I knelt down before the Communion rail, in the middle of the chapel, to recite the prayers of the Angel [the prayers[131] which

---

131   The angel taught the children these two prayers:
      "My God, I believe in Thee, I adore Thee, I hope in Thee, and I love Thee! I ask pardon of Thee for all those who do not believe in Thee, who do not adore Thee, who do not hope in Thee, and who do not love Thee!"
      "Most Holy Trinity, Father, Son, and Holy Ghost, I adore Thee profoundly. I offer Thee the most precious Body, Blood, Soul, and Divinity of the same Son, Jesus Christ, present in all the tabernacles of the world, in

Our Lady's precursor, St. Michael the Archangel, had taught to the children in his apparitions to them in 1916], lying prostrate. Feeling tired, I got up and knelt, and continued to recite them with my arms in the form of a cross. The only light came from the sanctuary lamp.

"Suddenly a supernatural light illumined the whole chapel, and on the altar there appeared a cross of light which reached the ceiling. In a brighter part, on the upper part of the Cross, could be seen the face of a man and His body to the waist; on His chest was an equally luminous dove; and nailed to the Cross, the body of another man. A little below the waist (of the latter), suspended in mid-air, could be seen a Chalice and a large Host, onto which fell some drops of Blood from the face of the Crucified One and from the wound in His breast. These drops ran down over the Host and fell into the Chalice.

"Under the right arm of the Cross was Our Lady with Her Immaculate Heart in Her hand… (It was Our Lady of Fatima with Her Immaculate Heart…in Her left hand…without a sword or roses, but with a crown of thorns and flames…) Under the left arm [of the Cross], some large letters, as it were of crystal-clear water flowing down over the Altar, formed these words: 'Grace and Mercy.'

"I understood that it was the mystery of the Most Holy Trinity that was shown to me, and I received lights about this mystery which I am not permitted to reveal.

"Then Our Lady said to me: '*The moment has come in which God asks the Holy Father to make, in union with all the bishops of the world, the consecration of Russia to My Immaculate Heart, **promising to save it by this means**. So numerous are the souls which the justice of God condemns for its sins committed against Me, that I come to ask for reparation. Sacrifice yourself for this intention and pray*.'"[132]

We see here (among other things) from Our Lady's further description of the Consecration of Russia, that Russia will be saved *by means of* this Consecration. This gives us a better understanding of how it will be that the Consecration itself establishes in the world the devotion to the Immaculate Heart of Mary.

---

reparation for all the sacrileges, outrages, and indifferences by which He is offended. And through the infinite merits of His most Sacred Heart, and the Immaculate Heart of Mary, I beg of Thee the conversion of poor sinners."

[132]   Père António Maria Martins, S.J., *Fatima, Documentos*, Porto, 1976, pp. 463-465, cited in Frère Michel de la Sainte Trinité, *The Whole Truth About Fatima*, Volume II, Immaculate Heart Publications, Buffalo, New York, 1989, pp. 463-464.

Russia, once the military, propaganda and control center of the great evils which have now spread throughout the world (bringing indescribable miseries in their wake, particularly to the nations which had already fallen under the yoke of terrors in Communist rule), will be miraculously converted back to the service of Christ by means of this Consecration. The relation of cause and effect will be apparent to all — to the amazement of the whole world, and to the great glory of Our Lady's Immaculate Heart, Whose coming Triumph has been predicted since Old Testament times. Father Gruner explains:

"The Consecration of Russia will serve two purposes. Just as the first purpose of an exorcism is to get rid of the demons of Satan that molest a person, the Consecration will rid Russia of the various diabolic errors and 'isms' that had been imported there. Russia, as a nation (both individually and with all of its institutions), will be miraculously converted.

"But there is a second purpose to this Consecration, which is to dedicate Russia to the service of the Immaculate Heart of Mary. And when the Russian nation has been set apart as Our Lady's own possession, She will use it to overcome the demonic and human beasts of the world that are fighting against God.

"Our Lady has told us that God wills to establish in the world devotion to the Immaculate Heart of Mary. God wants everyone to see Her power. And so He wants this public event, this public victory of the conversion of Russia to be seen to have come from the hands of the Blessed Virgin. The singular grace of conversion given to Russia will be seen to have come not just through the obedience of the Pope and the bishops, but particularly through the merits and intercession of the Immaculate Heart of Mary. That will strike the whole world in a way that will not be forgotten for centuries.

"By its conversion, Russia will become a powerhouse of evangelization at the service of the Blessed Virgin, so that the whole world will be converted to the True Faith. It is implicit in the Fatima Message, in the promise of a period of peace, that the whole world will become Catholic, shortly after this Consecration. And we see this predicted also in Sacred Scripture, in the second chapter of Isaias, where it is said: 'Come and let us go up to the mountain of the Lord, and to the house of God, and He will teach us His ways.' And all the nations come flooding into the Lord's house, the Catholic Church.

"The same passage in Isaias, along with other Old Testament prophecies, goes on to describe the universal peace that will follow the conversion of the nations: 'They shall turn their swords into ploughshares, and their spears into sickles: nation shall not lift up sword against nation, neither shall they be exercised any more to war' (Isaias 2:4). That is, they will turn their instruments of war into methods for producing food, and the art of war will not even be taught to the next generation. In another place, Isaias describes a time when the lion will lie down with the lamb and the lamb will not be hurt. (Isaias 11:6) The prophet Micheas repeats Isaias' prophecy of worldwide conversion and peace: 'People shall flow into the House of the Lord, and many nations shall come in haste, and say: Come, let us go up to the mountain of the Lord, and to the House of the God of Jacob, and He will teach us His ways. … And they shall beat their swords into ploughshares, and their spears into spades: nation shall not take sword against nation: neither shall they learn war anymore' (Micheas 4:3).

"In the whole six thousand years of recorded history, we've had more than 14,400 wars. That is more than two wars every year for the whole history of mankind. Our Lady of Fatima has promised to bring that era to an end, completely."[133]

Russia, and Russia Alone

With good reason, Our Lady of Fatima has requested that Russia specifically, and only Russia, be consecrated to Her Immaculate Heart. The consecration of a well-defined territory and people, as opposed to a general blessing invoked upon all nations, will allow the whole world to recognize that specific nation's sudden and miraculous collective conversion as an immediate effect of its consecration.

People will marvel at this relationship between the simple act of honoring the Immaculate Heart of Mary and the complete reversal of the world situation. It will be a glorious and public Triumph of Our Lady's Immaculate Heart, and it will lead to establishing great devotion to the Immaculate Heart of Mary everywhere in the world.

Also, since the Consecration of Russia will involve an act of faith and obedience on the part of the Pope and the bishops to Our Lady of Fatima's request, the divine authority possessed by the Catholic Church's hierarchy will be emphasized. The conversion of Russia and the gift of peace for the world will be clearly recognized as the marvelous and glorious result of the Pope's order to the bishops to join him in exercising this authority, in obedience to Our Lady of Fatima. The conversion of other nations throughout the world will spontaneously follow this dramatic proof that all graces come to mankind from God, not just through the Sacred humanity of Jesus Christ, but also through the Blessed Virgin Mary, and finally through the Catholic Church.

Father Gruner explains:

---

[133] Father Nicholas Gruner, "Fatima and Our Lady's Immaculate Heart," *Fatima: Only Way to World Peace* Conference speech, August 20, 2007; http://www.fatimapeaceconferences.com/brazil_2007/transcripts/fatima&olimh.pdf

"Why the Consecration of Russia? And why to the Immaculate Heart of Mary?

Sister Lucy has told us that, many times, the Blessed Virgin told her and her cousins Francisco and Jacinta that Russia is the instrument of chastisement that has been chosen by Heaven to punish the whole world (understood, for its sins) unless we obtain the conversion of that poor nation.

"God is going to be glorified in His Justice or in His Mercy. Even regimes that set themselves up to fight against God, still serve God's purposes. A Communist/Leninist regime enthroned itself in Moscow in 1917, and declared war on Christ and on His Church. God has allowed that. God has not only allowed it, God has a purpose behind it. What that purpose is, according to the Message of Fatima is, in justice, to punish the world for its sins.

"Nevertheless, God, in His Love for us, wants to manifest His Mercy, on the most generous terms. These terms are that the Pope and all the Catholic bishops, on the same day and at the same hour, consecrate (specifically) Russia to the Immaculate Heart of Mary.

"God's response, if they will do that, will be to say: 'For this little act of obedience, for this little act of reparation — for this little act of public acknowledgment, that I, God, have been blasphemously insulted by this upstart regime which uses My creation and My people to fight against Me around the world — I will manifest My Power. I will convert Russia to the Catholic faith, and give peace to the whole world.'

"Why specifically Russia, and Russia alone, and not the whole world?[134] As Sister Lucy says, 'Russia is a very well-defined territory.' In other words, we all know where the border is, and everyone knows who and where the Russian people are. So when Russia, specifically, is consecrated, and then the Russian people collectively and their institutions are converted from

---

[134] On March 25, 1984, Pope John Paul II consecrated *the world, not Russia* in particular, to Our Lady (unfortunately also, not precisely to the Immaculate Heart of Mary). In June 2000, Cardinal Bertone insisted that this consecration "corresponded to what Our Lady wished," adding, "Hence any further discussion or request is without basis."

Sister Lucy herself had said the opposite.

Having been presented a copy of the text that the Holy Father would use, Lucy stated on March 22, 1984 (three days before the ceremony): "That consecration cannot have a decisive character. ... *Russia does not appear in it as the sole object of the consecration*." (Frère François de Marie des Anges, *Fatima: Tragedy and Triumph*, Immaculate Heart Publications, 1994, pp. 167-168)

More than a year passed before Lucia was allowed to comment publicly on the 1984 ceremony. At last in September 1985, Spain's chapter of the Blue Army published an interview with Sister Lucy in its official journal, *Sol de Fatima*. Asked, "So the consecration was not done as requested by Our Lady?", Lucy replied: *"No. Many bishops attached no importance to this act. ... There was no participation of all the bishops and there was no mention of Russia."*

opposing God and His true Church, to the purpose of glorifying God and promoting His love and promoting His gospel, this sudden, miraculous, complete conversion will be so impressive and dramatic that people will easily see that the only thing that could have brought it about is the act of faith and obedience of the Pope and the bishops to Our Lady of Fatima's request.

"At the same time, the authority and the prestige of the Pope and the Catholic bishops will be recognized. Our Lord gave this authority to His Apostles and their successors at His Ascension, saying: 'All authority is given to Me in Heaven and earth. Go forth and teach all nations.'

"Our Lord wants the prestige of the Pope and the bishops to be seen for what it is — not because of who they are, but because He wants the authority that He gave them to be recognized throughout the world. That is why He is reserving world peace to the act of the Pope and the bishops exercising their authority in consecrating a country — in God's name and with the authority that God gave them to do this. God will glorify the Pope and the bishops in this way, so that the world will recognize that all graces come from God, through the Sacred humanity of Jesus Christ, through the Blessed Virgin, then through the Catholic Church, to mankind.

"This conversion of Russia will be the major turning point in the history of mankind for all time to come. That's why it has to be a specific country, and that's why it is to be that specific country of Russia."[135]

On the Verge of an Historic Change

Our Lady told little Lucy in 1917 that Jesus wanted to leave her in the world for some time, in order to use her to make Our Lady known and loved. It is clear from these words that up until this point, throughout all of the Church's history, the Immaculate Heart of Mary has not been well-enough known and loved, in God's view — the only one that counts.

At last this deficiency is about to be remedied, to some degree at least, by God Himself. God is about to establish in the world devotion to the Immaculate Heart of Mary, such as it has never before existed. This unparalleled level of devotion will come about as an expression of gratitude and praise to Our Lady when people finally realize what inestimable power and grace and goodness the Blessed Virgin has, when She is clearly seen by all to have saved the world from enslavement to tyrants (and ultimately to the devil).

Such an enslavement is even now well underway. The Mystery of Iniquity has

---

[135]   Father Nicholas Gruner, "The Secret of Padre Pio" (Part II), *The Fatima Crusader*, Issue 63; http://www.fatimacrusader.com/cr63/cr63pg32.asp

already thoroughly established itself in the world, and if Our Lady's intervention is put off much longer, the whole world will soon be utterly subjected to a satanic tyranny worse than anything ever seen before.

For the moment, and for as long as the Consecration of Russia is delayed, God will not let Our Lady use Her power — the power that She has, all by Herself, to stop all wars; the power that She has to prevent, by Her own merits alone, the punishments that God would otherwise inflict upon the world for its sins. God wants to give us the unmerited blessing of world peace, but He insists that the Immaculate Heart of Mary gets the credit for it.

When the Consecration is finally performed, it will overflow in glory to Our Lady's Immaculate Heart. Father Gruner continues:

"We have the teaching of both St. Bernard and St. Alphonsus that if we want our offering to be accepted by God, we must be sure to offer it through the hands of the Blessed Virgin.

"There are many things which are imperfect in our own hearts, and in our gifts. If we make an offering on our own, God of course sees all these imperfections. But He finds no imperfections whatsoever in the Immaculate Conception. There is no imperfection in Her, and every prayer and offering that She makes is unimaginably powerful before God — just because it comes from Her.

"In this command for the Consecration of Russia, God is saying to us, 'I want you to rededicate this country back to My service, but rededicate it to Me through the Immaculate Heart of Mary.'

"Another reason, given in the Message of Fatima itself, for why God insists that this consecration be made to the Immaculate Heart of Mary, is that God wants Our Lady to get the credit for the miraculous conversion of Russia and for the world peace which follows.

"We live in one of the most sinful times in the history of the world. Never before have such terrible crimes been promoted and justified on such a wide scale. As Pope Pius XII taught in 1951, 'The world at this time is worse than before the flood.' Today is even worse still. We do not deserve the gift of world peace, but God in His love for us wants to give it to us.

"As Saint Augustine tells us, there are certain graces — certain favors, if you will — which God wants to give us, but which He knows we don't deserve. Nevertheless, God still wants to give them to us. So God has a dilemma, so to speak: 'How can I give these gifts to mankind when I know they don't deserve them? They are going to become proud. They are going to think that they somehow deserved this gift (of world peace, for instance).'

"Saint Augustine explains that God has found a way around this dilemma. God can give us these special, undeserved graces through the merits and intercession of the Saints. In this way, God gets to exercise His love and generosity to us by giving us things beyond our own merits, and we realize that we have received them not because we deserve them, but only because of the great merits and intercession of the Saints.

"In the Message of Fatima, we are told that God has entrusted the great Grace of world peace exclusively to the Immaculate Heart of Mary.

"Furthermore, God wants the whole world to recognize this.

"So God has laid down the condition: 'NO. You are not going to have peace, you're not going to have the conversion of Russia without the Blessed Virgin. It is by Her merits and Her prayers that this is going to take place. I will give it to you, I want to give it to you, but I will only do it through the merits and intercession of the Blessed Virgin Mary.'"[136]

We can begin to understand, then, why God insists upon this act — a specific, public solemn act of obedience in honor of the Immaculate Heart of Mary — and why otherwise He will not grant us world peace. As Our Lady told Sister Lucy in 1952:

"Make it known to the Holy Father that I still await the *consecration of Russia* to My Immaculate Heart. *Without this consecration* Russia cannot be converted, nor can the world have peace."[137]

We know that God will not change His mind (to use a human expression) about this. God's will, as Our Lady has said, is to establish in the world the devotion to Her Immaculate Heart, to such a degree as has never yet existed — and it is His fixed will that this be accomplished through the Consecration of Russia to that Immaculate Heart.

Every nation today stands in need of conversion,[138] and Russia's conversion will be the occasion of the conversion of all the other nations as well. The whole world will

---

[136] Father Nicholas Gruner, "The Secret of Padre Pio," (Part II), *The Fatima Crusader*, Issue 63; http://www.fatimacrusader.com/cr63/cr63pg32.asp

[137] Reported in the Italian bishops' publication, *Il pellegrinaggio delle meraviglie*, 1960, p.440. Cited in Frère Michel, *The Whole Truth About Fatima,* Vol. III, p. 327. Emphasis added.

[138] Our Lord drew attention to this fact in a 1931 revelation to Sister Lucy, in which He taught her two prayers by which she was to pray for the conversion of the whole world. Sister Lucy relates the incident in her August 29, 1931 letter to her bishop: "My confessor orders me to inform Your Excellency of what took place a little while ago between the Good Lord and myself: As I was asking God for the conversion of Russia, Spain, and Portugal, it seemed to me that His Divine Majesty said to me: 'You console Me a great deal by asking Me for the conversion of those poor nations. Ask it also of My Mother frequently, saying: "*Sweet Heart of Mary, be the salvation of Russia, Spain, Portugal, Europe, and the whole world.*" At other times say: "*By Thy pure and Immaculate Conception, O Mary, obtain for me the conversion of Russia, Spain, Portugal, Europe, and the entire world.*"'" (Cited in Frère Michel de la Sainte Trinité, *The Whole Truth About Fatima*, Volume II, Immaculate Heart Publications, Buffalo, New York, 1989, p. 543.)

recognize that it has been saved from a most cruel enslavement to diabolic powers, singlehandedly by Our Lady, Whose power is so much greater than the devil's, and Whose great merits have averted the terrible punishments due to the world.

This will be apparent to all, since Russia's Consecration to Our Lady's Immaculate Heart will be the clear occasion of its conversion — the direct cause, as Our Lady said, by means of which God will save Russia.

Our Lord Himself affirmed this to Sister Lucy in a revelation of 1936. Sister Lucy recounts:

"Intimately I have spoken to Our Lord about the subject, and not too long ago I asked Him why He would not convert Russia without the Holy Father making that consecration?

"'Because I want My whole Church *to acknowledge that Consecration as a Triumph* of the Immaculate Heart of Mary, so that it may extend Its cult later on, and place the devotion to this Immaculate Heart beside the devotion to My Sacred Heart.'"[139]

Father Nicholas Gruner, director of The Fatima Center, has dedicated his priestly life (38 years!) exclusively to promoting the Message of Fatima.
Our Lady of Fatima's words are very clear: "If My requests are heeded, Russia will be converted, and there will be peace." Father Gruner knew from the time that he first learned of the Fatima Message, that if Our Lady had not yet kept Her promise, the fault could not be Hers.

Establishing This Devotion in the World

The Consecration itself will be hailed throughout the whole world as a most glorious triumph of the Immaculate Heart over the powers of iniquity in this world.

Finally, the world will understand — in a way that it has never yet widely understood and appreciated — the great holiness, the great merits, and the great power, of the Immaculate Heart of Mary. This understanding will be the key to the salvation of the many souls who would otherwise be lost, as Our Lady indicated on July 13, 1917 —

---

[139]   Sister Lucy's letter of May 18, 1936 to Father José Gonçalves, cited in Frère Michel de la Sainte Trinité, *The Whole Truth About Fatima*, Volume II, Immaculate Heart Publications, Buffalo, New York, 1989, p. 631.

that by establishing in the world the devotion to the Immaculate Heart, God would save many sinners from going to hell.

The saints have often told us that no one who sincerely and perseveringly invokes the Blessed Virgin can be lost. It seems like an exaggeration, but it is not. She lived so well and is so full of merits that She could gain the salvation of every human being who will ever live. Father Gruner explains:

> "No matter how hard we work, we cannot, through our own efforts, bring about world peace. … It is not through the merits of all our hard work that we will get this grace. It is through the merits and intercession of the Blessed Virgin. That is why God has made it so easy for us [*i.e.*, through a simple (but solemn) five-minute prayer], so that everyone can see that it is not by our efforts but by the merits of Our Lady. …

> "We should not let this great truth pass us by, just because it seems so simple. It is only through the merits of the Blessed Virgin, through Her intercession, that the world will have peace.

> "St. Alphonsus tells us it is a great thing if a man is good enough to merit his own salvation. Apparently it doesn't happen very often. It is even a greater thing for a man or a woman to merit not only his or her own salvation but the salvation of others. That is what the saints have done.

> "It is the greatest thing of all for a mere human person to merit enough to save the souls of all mankind, and that only the Blessed Virgin Mary has done. So God wants Her to be honored, for Her own sake and for the love He has for Her, but also for our sake. God wants us to recognize how easy it is to save our souls by being devoted to the Blessed Virgin, by depending on Her merits and Her intercession."[140]

Most of us are far too weak and inconstant to make it to Heaven on our own, and many, many souls are going to hell, whereas they could be saved if only they understood the importance of devotion to the Blessed Virgin Mary. If only these souls would sincerely and perseveringly invoke Our Lady, they would be converted from their sins and preserved from the eternal chastisements of those sins that they fell into.

When this devotion to the Immaculate Heart is established in the world, sinners who would otherwise be lost will be saved. And this devotion will ultimately be established by the Consecration of Russia, which will demonstrate Our Lady's glory like no other miracle ever witnessed before, because She will be seen to have personally intervened to stop the most cruel wars and persecutions.

---

140   Father Nicholas Gruner, "The Consecration of Russia or the Annihilation of Nations and Enslavement of the World: The Choice is Yours," speech delivered at the *Last Chance for World Peace* conference in Tuy, Spain, on October 12, 2006; http://www.fatimapeaceconferences.com/spainport06/transcripts/fg_6.asp

Waging Peace

Our Lord wept over Jerusalem because the city did not recognize its hour. This is our hour, and our time is short. We have an obligation to look at the facts and to accept the truth — the truth, first of all, that we are quickly headed toward war, and secondly, that *we have been given the means to change our course and stop the coming war.*

President John F. Kennedy faced down his war-hungry Joint Chiefs of Staff when they were clamoring for a murderous assault on Russia, and again when they presented him with a murderous plan for instigating a war in Cuba. He was infuriated by their program for U.S. hegemony at the cost of innocent lives, and he rejected that godless program of his day.

We today have inherited that same program, now in full force. We, too, need to reject it and to ***stop it***.

How can we stop the wars and other machinations of those who are in the process of imposing a Masonic New World Order upon us, when even a U.S. President was unable to make a successful stand[141] against them?

Certainly not by our own power or efforts.

Pope Benedict XV (who was reigning throughout World War I) used every political and diplomat means available to the Church in order to stop World War I. By May 5, 1917, he realized that no merely human means could bring the "suicide of civilized Europe" to an end. On that date he formally directed the bishops and faithful to beg the grace of peace from Our Lady, the Queen of Peace and Mediatrix of all graces.

Today, we know even more than Pope Benedict XV did. We know not only that we are powerless of ourselves to stop the coming war, and that this grace can come only through Our Lady. We also know from Our Lady Herself, Who answered the Pope's call by coming to Fatima eight days later on May 13, 1917, that *God will grant this grace of peace only when we ask it through the merits of the Immaculate Heart of Mary.* On a special day of worldwide prayer and reparation, the Holy Father must make, and order all the Catholic bishops of the world to make with him, the Consecration of Russia to the Immaculate Heart of Mary.

As Our Lady told Sister Lucy, God promises to convert Russia *by means of this Consecration.* Our Lady has also assured us that there is no other possible means of securing the conversion of Russia or peace in the world: "Only Our Lady of the Rosary can help you," She told the children on July 13, 1917.

Many people, including many journalists, see the looming disaster of war and more war, and even of a nuclear holocaust, and they ask, "What can we do?"

Yes, there is a war brewing — a war which promises to be far more terrible than any of the other incessant wars that have plagued the world since 1917. But we also have the answer to this problem. Our Lady has given us the means to save our lives, and (more importantly) to save many souls who will otherwise be lost without the graces of

---

141   Executive Order 11110, JFK's attempt to reform the monetary and banking system on which the New World Order is being constructed, may have been the single greatest factor leading to his assassination. *Cf.* John P. Curran, "JFK vs. The Federal Reserve"; http://www.rense.com/general76/jfkvs.htm

On May 13, 1917, Our Lady of Fatima appeared to three shepherd children, asking them: "Are you willing to offer yourselves to God and to bear all the sufferings He wills to send you, as an act of reparation [for the sins by which He is offended, and of supplication] for the conversion of sinners? … Pray the Rosary every day, in order to obtain peace for the world, and the end of the war."

conversion and world peace that the Consecration will bring.

The remedy to our problems is close at hand; we simply need to employ it in order for conversion and peace to follow as *divinely promised effects*.

How to Move the Pope to Obey Our Lady

It is true that only the Pope can give the necessary order to the bishops to join him in making the Consecration of Russia. Nevertheless, it is in our power to bring about the Church's obedience to this request of Our Lady of Fatima.

How can we move the Pope to obey Our Lord's command (announced through Our Lady of Fatima) for the Consecration of Russia? Or if he will not be moved, how can we get a better Pope — the Pope we need, who will obey Our Lady?

Sister Lucy had the same question, even as far back as 1936. At that time, seven long years had already passed since Our Lady's solemn and urgent request of June 13, 1929 in Tuy, Spain, for the Consecration of Russia — when, as Our Lady said, *the moment* had come that God asked for the Consecration to be made, without delay. Still, seven years later in 1936, there had been no indication of progress toward moving Pius XI (the Pope at that time) to respond to this command from Heaven.

Sister Lucy was rather perplexed, and she wondered what could be done. She asked Our Lord — in fact, she all but objected to Him that the project was hopeless:

"But my God, the Holy Father probably won't believe me, unless You Yourself move him with a special inspiration."

Our Lord's reply to Lucy is the answer to our own question as well, since we remain in the same predicament to this day:[142]

"The Holy Father. *Pray much for the Holy Father!*"[143]

Our prayers for the Holy Father can obtain the efficacious graces that we need for the Pope to finally obey.

But it might be objected that the Holy Father has a free will. What if he refuses the graces proffered to him and does not allow himself to be moved to believe and obey Our Lady's Message?

Our prayers will not go unanswered, as the prophet Jeremias assures us:

"*Return*, O ye revolting children, ... and *I will give you pastors according to My own heart*"[144]

Our conversion and prayers will infallibly bring about whatever is needed for our preservation, even if that requires new pastors in place of the old. Father Gruner comments on this passage:

---

[142]   That is, after 85 years of despising the Fatima Message, to the virtual ruin of both the Church and society!

[143]   Sister Lucy's letter of May 18, 1936 to Father José Gonçalves, cited in Frère Michel de la Sainte Trinité, *The Whole Truth About Fatima*, Volume II, Immaculate Heart Publications, Buffalo, New York, 1989, p. 631. Emphasis added.

[144]   Jeremias 3: 14-15

"The first way to stop the wholesale stealing (closing) of our churches is to pray and make sacrifices for our pastors, so that God sends us good pastors. God can remove a bad pastor by taking away his life or his health, or by converting him. If the pastor will be converted, that's great. But if not, God will remove him and send you pastors after His own heart. So in that sense the pastors we have, and the decisions they have made over the last 40 years, are in part, if not altogether, a reflection on the Catholic faithful."[145]

Our Own Part in This Mess

So the original question of how we can move the Pope to obey Our Lord's command finally leads us back to another question: Why has the Church and the world been made to suffer the consequences of having a series of Popes who have refused to believe and/or properly obey the Message of Fatima? How did we come to get such Popes (and pastors of all ranks, for that matter)? These pastors who have cooperated in our impending ruin by their silence or even misrepresentations of the Message of Fatima have up to now failed us critically, like those who have brought shame onto the Church by some public crime.

How did we come to get such godless political leaders as we have had in recent years, who have led us so far down the path away from our salvation?

Saint John Eudes explains this for us, referring us back to the same passage from Jeremias that we just noted:

"The most evident mark of God's anger and the most terrible castigation He can inflict upon the world are manifested when He permits His people to fall into the hands of clergy who are priests more in name than in deed, priests who practice the cruelty of ravening wolves rather than charity and affection of devoted shepherds....

"When God permits such things, it is a very positive proof that He is thoroughly angry with His people, and is visiting His most dreadful anger upon them. That is why He cries unceasingly to Christians, 'Return, O ye revolting children, ... and I will give you pastors according to My own heart.' Thus, irregularities in the lives of priests constitute a scourge upon the people in consequence of sin."[146]

Father Gruner explains:

"I know we didn't do it personally, but we in some way are responsible [for the present condition of the Church's hierarchy], for as St. John Eudes explains, God sends bad clergy as a punishment.

---

[145]   Father Nicholas Gruner, "Our Lady of Fatima Warned Us About: The Dangers to the Faith and to the Life of the Christian," *The Fatima Crusader*, Issue 93, p. 57; http://www.fatimacrusader.com/cr93/cr93pg3.pdf

[146]   St. John Eudes, *The Priest: His Dignity and Obligations*, Kenedy & Sons, New York, 1947, reprinted by Immaculate Heart Publications, Buffalo, New York, pp. 9-10.

"St. John Eudes explains that Jeremias speaks for God, saying, 'If you, My people, will turn back to Me, then I (God) will send you pastors after My own heart.'

"That is, if you turn back to God by your lives, by your penance, then God will send good priests to take care of your souls. On the other hand, if you do not turn back to God, then God will send you bad pastors — pastors who will not shepherd your soul, but instead will lead you to hell (if you follow them). That is the worst chastisement that God can inflict on His people."[147]

Father's point holds true in the larger picture — we surely have the civil leadership that we deserve. One Western nation after another has succumbed to the institutionalizing of outrageously sinful practices, with far too meager a voice raised in protest or in public reparation. Too often as well, Catholics themselves have given way to the impulse of a false patriotism that says, "My country, right or wrong!" or "My party's leadership, no matter what its platforms!"

The terrible problems that we face within the Church and in society at large, then, are rooted in our own infidelities. We have ourselves to blame. And as Father Gruner has often pointed out, this pertains particularly to *the degree to which we have responded to Our Lady of Fatima with the honor and obedience due to Her Message*, as the singular intervention of Heaven for our time. This ties in directly with the scourge of bad pastors spoken of by Saint John Eudes, as we are about to see.

Sister Lucy spoke about the Third Secret of Fatima in terms of a frightful punishment from God falling down upon the faithful without their being aware of it, in the form of a dissipated and corrupted clergy in the Church. Our failing hierarchy is a punishment from God for the great majority of the faithful who themselves have paid no attention to Our Lady of Fatima! Speaking to Father Fuentes, she said:

"Father, the Most Holy Virgin is very sad because no one has paid any attention to Her Message, neither the good nor the bad. The good continue on their way but without giving any importance to Her Message. The bad, not seeing the punishment of God actually falling upon them, continue their life of sin without even caring about the message. But believe me, Father, God will chastise the world and this will be in a terrible manner. The punishment from Heaven is imminent. …

"[T]he devil is in the mood for engaging in a decisive battle against the Blessed Virgin. And the devil knows what it is that most offends God and which in a short space of time will gain for him the greatest number of souls. Thus the devil does everything to overcome souls consecrated to God because in this way, the devil will succeed in leaving the souls of the faithful

---

147   Father Nicholas Gruner, "Our Lady of Fatima Warned Us About: The Dangers to the Faith and to the Life of the Christian," *The Fatima Crusader*, Issue 93, p. 57; http://www.fatimacrusader.com/cr93/cr93pg3.pdf

abandoned by their leaders; thereby the more easily will he seize them.

"That which afflicts the Immaculate Heart of Mary and the (Sacred) Heart of Jesus is the fall of religious and priestly souls. The devil knows that religious and priests who fall away from their beautiful vocation drag numerous souls to hell.

"The devil wishes to take possession of consecrated souls. He tries to corrupt them in order to lull to sleep the souls of lay people and thereby lead them to final impenitence. He employs all tricks, even going so far as to suggest the delay of entrance into religious life. Resulting from this is the sterility of the interior life, and among the lay people, coldness (lack of enthusiasm) regarding the subject of renouncing pleasures and the total dedication of themselves to God."[148]

Sister Lucy said above that when the faithful had been abandoned by their leaders, the devil would in many cases be easily able to seize them. In other words, then, by despising the Message of Fatima, the faithful have not only left their pastors open to a furious attack by the devil, but have also opened themselves up to being dragged to hell along with their defecting pastors. Father Gruner explains:

"What is this punishment Sister Lucy spoke of? ... [I]t takes the eyes of faith to see it. By that I do not mean faith in Our Lady's Message, but rather understanding Her Message from the perspective of the Catholic Faith. ...

"We see that our Catholic Faith has become comfortable, that the Cross is no longer there, that we no longer have to make any sacrifices.

"One person told me, 'I really don't like this brand of Catholicism because it doesn't please me, so I just put it aside.' They think they can pick and choose. I've had people tell me they go to Confessor A and, if he tells them something they don't want to hear, they go to Confessor B, because they know he is going to be much softer.

"God is not going to be mocked. ...

"The chastisement that has been visited upon us shows that the devil has had his chance and has succeeded. He has succeeded not only with the 55,000 priests who left the ministry [between the years 1965 and 1975], but with all those who have bought into the modernist interpretation of the Scriptures, Liturgy and even dogma — and the modernist interpretation of Fatima.

---

[148] December 26, 1957 interview with Fr. Augustin Fuentes, cited in Frère Michel de la Sainte Trinité, *The Whole Truth About Fatima*, Volume III, Immaculate Heart Publications, Buffalo, New York, pp. 504-505.

"I must confess that when I read St. Pius X's encyclical on Modernism,[149] I was very frightened. I was flying from London back to Canada to enter the seminary, when I read in his encyclical some of the devious and devilish tricks that the modernists use.

"One of these terrible tricks is to redefine Catholic terms. When they use the word "transubstantiation" or "magisterium" or any other Catholic word, they apply a new meaning to that word, but they don't do you the favor or have the honesty of telling you they have redefined the term. They just use it over and over and over again [in this altered sense], and eventually you come to redefine the term in your own mind, and you stop thinking like a Catholic."[150]

Father Gruner continues, in another place:

"St. John Eudes explains that the most terrible chastisement God can send to His people is bad priests (which obviously includes bad bishops, Cardinals and could include even a pope). ...

"[Today] we have the infiltration of all kinds of corrupt people into the priesthood. It is obvious that God is very angry with His people because of all the bad priests we now see in the Church, most visibly in the clerical scandals. ... But those scandals are not limited to perverted and corrupt priests and bishops. Worse yet is the corruption of our Catholic faith by so-

Sister Lucy, the last surviving seer of the Fatima apparitions, was interviewed by Father Augustin Fuentes, the postulator of the cause for the beatification of the other two seers, Francisco and Jacinta Marto, on December 26, 1957 (ten years before this 1967 photograph was taken). It was in this historic interview that Sister Lucy said, "The Most Holy Virgin is very sad because no one has paid any attention to Her Message."

For the final 45 years of her life, Sister Lucy was essentially silenced by Vatican officials. Even as of 1957, interviews with Sister Lucy were rarely granted. By 1960, even Sister Lucy's previous confessor was denied access to her.

Father Fuentes' interview was therefore perhaps the last unrestricted interview with Sister Lucy that was ever published — the last unvarnished, un-retouched interview that Sister Lucy ever gave.

149   *Pascendi Dominici Gregis*, 1907.

150   Father Nicholas Gruner, "Sister Lucy's Last Unrestricted Interview," *Last Chance for World Peace* conference speech given in Tuy, Spain, October 9, 2006; http://www.fatimapeaceconferences.com/ spainport06/transcripts/fg_4.asp

called 'defenders' of the Faith.

"Those who claim the 'living Magisterium' takes precedence over the infallible, unchangeable dogmatic definitions are leading countless souls to hell. The perversion by priests, bishops and Cardinals who tell us that there is no need for unbelievers to convert to the Catholic Faith[151] is a greater perversion than pedophilia — as horrid as pedophilia is. This heresy — even if it is promoted by Vatican Cardinals, even if it were to have the support, implicit or explicit, of the Pope — does not change one bit the perversity of such teaching.

"Those who defend such teaching of the 'living Magisterium' have either lost their faith, or have been completely ignorant of it all their lives. But their ignorance does not necessarily excuse them from grievous sin in this matter."[152]

The Role of Satan and his Allies in this Mess

It is our own crimes, then, that have brought such a terrible punishment upon us, but to tell the whole story, we have been equally the victims of the crimes of others on our way to this point.

The subversion and corruption of the Christian West has been a centuries-long, calculated project of the enemies of the Church — namely, of Freemasonry, and of its daughter-system, Communism.[153] It required more than a dagger, as Freemasonry realized,

---

[151]   This dogma of Faith, that outside of the Catholic Church there is no salvation, has been solemnly and infallibly defined three times:

"There is but one universal Church of the faithful, outside which no one at all is saved." (Pope Innocent III, A.D. 1215, at the Fourth Lateran Council)

"We declare, say, define, and pronounce that it is absolutely necessary for the salvation of every human creature to be subject to the Roman Pontiff." (Pope Boniface VIII, A.D. 1302, in the Bull *Unam Sanctam*)

"The most Holy Roman Church firmly believes, professes and preaches that none of those existing outside the Catholic Church, not only pagans, but also Jews and heretics and schismatics, can have a share in life eternal; but that they will go into the eternal fire which was prepared for the devil and his angels, unless before death they are joined with Her; and that so important is the unity of this ecclesiastical body that only those remaining within this unity can profit by the sacraments of the Church unto salvation, and they alone can receive an eternal recompense for their fasts, their almsgivings, their other works of Christian piety and the duties of a Christian soldier. No one, let his almsgiving be as great as it may, no one, even if he pour out his blood for the Name of Christ, can be saved, unless he remain within the bosom and the unity of the Catholic Church." (Pope Eugene IV, A.D. 1442, in the Bull *Cantate Domino*)

[152]   Father Nicholas Gruner, "Truth Does Not Change: If We Lose Dogma, We Lose Our Soul," Fatima News and Views, January 30, 2014, p. 4; http://www.fatima.org/news/newsviews/newsviews013014.pdf

[153]   In his article, "The Frankfurt School: Conspiracy to Corrupt," Timothy Matthews gives this description of the Communist's Frankfurt School:

"Towards the end of 1922, ...on Lenin's initiative a meeting [of] the Communist International (Comintern)... was organized at the Marx-Engels Institute in Moscow. The aim of the meeting was to clarify the concept of, and give concrete effect to, a Marxist cultural revolution. Amongst those present were Georg Lukacs (a Hungarian aristocrat, the son of a banker, who had become a Communist during World War I — a good Marxist theoretician, he developed the idea of 'Revolution and Eros': sexual instinct used as an instrument of destruction) and Willi Munzenberg (whose proposed solution was to 'organize the intellectuals and use them to make Western civilization stink. Only then, after they have corrupted all its values and made

to remove the Catholic Church as an obstacle to their plans. As soon as one Pope was killed, another would be elected in his place. In order to bring down the papacy and the entire Catholic Church with it, what was needed was *the corruption of Christian hearts*. In this way, as Father Denis Fahey points out,[154] they would poison the well from which future generations of Catholics were drawn, by lowering the ideals of future priests and educators, and by corrupting the future mothers of families. Freemasonry itself has published its aim:

"Let us spread vice broadcast among the multitude. Let them breathe it through their five senses, let them drink it in and become saturated with it. … Make men's hearts corrupt and vicious and you will have no more Catholics. Draw away priests from their work, from the altar and from the practice of virtue. Strive skillfully to fill their minds and occupy their time with other matters. …

"Recently one of our friends, laughing at our projects, said to us: 'To overcome the Catholic Church, you must begin by suppressing the female sex.' There is a certain sense in which the words are true; but since we cannot suppress woman, let us corrupt her along with the Church. … The best poniard with which to wound the Church mortally is corruption."[155]

It was a strategy as old as the Old Testament prophet Balaam, who, as St. John says, "taught Balac to cast a stumbling block before the children of Israel, to eat things sacrificed to idols, and to commit fornication."[156]

True to their word, Masonry has cunningly introduced all manner of evils, intellectual and moral, into the fabric of our lives. And as Our Lady of Fatima warned, these scandals did indeed come by active design: "Russia *will spread its errors* throughout the world," and "certain fashions *will be introduced* which will give great offense to God."

---

life impossible, can we impose the dictatorship of the proletariat'). 'It was,' said Ralph de Toledano (the conservative author and co-founder of the *National Review*), a meeting 'perhaps more harmful to Western civilization than the Bolshevik Revolution itself.'" (Published in *Catholic Insight*, March 2009 issue, online at http://www.whale.to/c/frankfurt_school1.html and http://www.freerepublic.com/focus/news/2216734/posts)

[154]   Rev. Denis Fahey, C.S.Sp., *The Kingship of Christ and the Conversion of the Jewish Nation*, 1953; http://www.catholicapologetics.info/apologetics/judaism/conversion.htm

[155]   Instructions of the Italian Masonic Alta Vendita in *L'Eglise Romaine en face de la Révolution*, by Crétineau-Joly, Vol. II, pp. 128-129; cited in Rev. Denis Fahey, C.S.Sp., *The Kingship of Christ and the Conversion of the Jewish Nation*.

[156]   Apocalypse 2: 14. The story of Balaam is told in the Book of Numbers, Chapters 22-24. The prophet Balaam would gladly have pronounced a curse upon the people of Israel for the sake of money offered by Balac, the king of the Moab, if God had allowed him to do so. Instead, still hoping to please the king, Balaam gave him the wicked advice of leading the Israelites to sin, after which they would no longer enjoy God's protection. So Balac sent immoral women to live among the Israelites and lead them into fornication and idolatry. The effect of this scandal, told in Chapter 25, was that 24,000 Israelite men were slain as a punishment from God: "And the people committed fornication with the daughters of Moab, who called them to their sacrifices. And they ate of them, and adored their gods. And … the Lord being angry, said to Moses: Take … and hang them up on gibbets against the sun, that My fury may be turned away from Israel."

It Is Not Too Late to Have Recourse to Jesus and Mary

The way out of our predicament, then, is to retrace our steps — to turn back, to correct ourselves, and to make reparation for our crimes. Sister Lucy has told us of Our Lord's insistent desire that we make reparation and that we pray for ourselves and others:

"God is resolved to purify in their blood all the nations which want to destroy His kingdom in souls; and yet He promises to be appeased and grant pardon, if people pray and do penance."[157]

In another place, she adds:

"[S]ince now is the hour of God's justice over the world, we need to apply ourselves continually to prayer. For this reason I feel that it would be good to impress on people, in addition to a great amount of confidence in the mercy of Our Good Lord and in the protection of the Immaculate Heart of Mary, *the need for prayer accompanied by sacrifice*, especially the sacrifices needed to avoid sin. ... [I]n the state that the world is in now, what Our Lord wants are souls who, *united with Him, will pray and sacrifice themselves*. ... Now more than ever *He needs souls who will give themselves to Him without reserve — and how small this number is!*"[158]

Most significantly, in August 1931, Our Lord gave us an explicit guarantee of His attentiveness to our prayers, no matter how far advanced our plight. Sister Lucy recalls first how displeased Our Lord was because His request had not been attended to,[159] and how He "complainingly said to [her] by means of an interior communication":

"They did not want to heed My request. ... [T]hey will repent and do so, but it will be late. Russia will already have spread her errors throughout the world, causing wars and persecutions of the Church. The Holy Father will have much to suffer!"[160]

But in this same communication, Our Lord immediately goes on to add this all-important assurance:

"It will never be too late to have recourse to Jesus and Mary."[161]

Even at this very late hour, when already so much has been lost, still our repentance and reparation can move Heaven to avert the coming war.

---

[157] Letter to the Bishop of Leiria, October 24, 1939, cited in Frère Michel de la Sainte Trinité, *The Whole Truth About Fatima*, Volume II, Immaculate Heart Publications, Buffalo, New York, 1989, p. 685.

[158] Letter of August 18, 1940 to Father José Gonçalves, (emphasis added), cited in Frère Michel de la Sainte Trinité, *The Whole Truth About Fatima*, Volume II, Immaculate Heart Publications, Buffalo, New York, 1989, pp. 727-728.

[159] Cf. Letter of January 21, 1935 to Father José Gonçalves, cited in Frère Michel de la Sainte Trinité, *The Whole Truth About Fatima*, Volume II, Immaculate Heart Publications, Buffalo, New York, 1989, p. 544.

[160] Letter of May 1936 to Father José Gonçalves, cited in Frère Michel de la Sainte Trinité, *The Whole Truth About Fatima*, Volume II, Immaculate Heart Publications, Buffalo, New York, 1989, p. 544.

[161] Letter of August 29, 1931 to her bishop, cited in Frère Michel de la Sainte Trinité, *The Whole Truth About Fatima*, Volume II, Immaculate Heart Publications, Buffalo, New York, 1989, p. 544.

Our Lady of Fatima asks us to practice the reparatory devotions to Her Immaculate Heart. "Look, My daughter, at My Heart, surrounded with thorns with which ungrateful men pierce Me at every moment by their blasphemies and ingratitude. Do you, at least, try to console Me and announce in My name that I promise to assist at the moment of death, with all the graces necessary for salvation, all those who, on the first Saturday of five consecutive months shall confess, receive Holy Communion, recite five decades of the Rosary, and keep Me company for fifteen minutes while meditating on the fifteen mysteries of the Rosary, with the intention of making reparation to Me. ... So numerous are the souls which the justice of God condemns for sins committed against Me, that I have come to ask for reparation."

Devotions to the
Immaculate Heart of Mary

As Sister Lucy told Father Fuentes, in our time, God has attached a greater efficacy to the prayer of the Holy Rosary than it has ever had. Our daily Rosaries, along with our other prayers and sacrifices, can move Heaven:

"The Most Holy Virgin in these last times in which we live has given a new efficacy to the recitation of the Rosary to such an extent that there is no problem, no matter how difficult it is, whether temporal or above all, spiritual, in the personal life of each one of us, of our families, of the families of the world, or of the religious communities, or *even of the life of peoples and nations*, that cannot be solved by the Rosary. *There is no problem, I tell you, no matter how difficult it is, that we cannot resolve by the prayer of the Holy Rosary*. With the Holy Rosary, we will save ourselves. We will sanctify ourselves. We will console Our Lord and obtain the salvation of many souls. ...

"Tell them also, Father, that my cousins Francisco and Jacinta sacrificed themselves because in all the apparitions of the Most Holy Virgin, they always saw Her very sad. She never smiled at us. This sadness, this anguish which we noted in Her penetrated our souls. This sadness is caused by the offenses against God and the punishments which menace sinners. And so, we children did not know what to think except to invent various means of praying and making sacrifices."[162]

Even now, a campaign of prayer, penance, and reparation for sins can save us. We need to beg Our Lord for the fulfillment of Heaven's request for the Consecration of Russia. We need to pray for our leaders, and to pray for the Pope. We need to pray especially that God will no longer allow Our Lady of Fatima's Message (our only hope!) to be buried, hidden, and despised.

Let us get on our knees and ask for these graces from Our Lady, particularly through the reparatory devotions which She urged upon us in Her Fatima apparitions: Wearing the Brown Scapular at all times; praying at least five decades of the Holy Rosary each day; making the First Saturday Communion of Reparation each month; and making the full First Saturdays devotion on five consecutive months at least once, but preferably many times. (Sister Lucy's practice was to begin a new set of First Saturdays as soon as she had finished the previous five.)[163]

We need to attach great importance to these devotions, and never to omit them! Our lives and many souls (possibly including our own and our loved ones') depend on our fidelity to these prayers. As Saint Padre Pio used to advise his clients, we need to pray the Rosary and get others to pray the Rosary! As Pope Pius XII reminds us, the Rosary has been given to us by Heaven as a sure remedy "for the healing of the evils which afflict our times."[164] And if we have truly given the Message of Fatima the central and urgent place that it deserves in our lives, then there should not be much difficulty or debate when we have to choose between a First Saturday Mass and Tommy's soccer game. (And one way or the other, we parents give a very clear message and lesson to Tommy by the priority that we choose to honor.)

Sister Lucy recorded two special promises extended to the world by Our Lady of Fatima within just a few months of each other in the spring of 1939, when World War II was already imminent — two promises made at that late hour, which undoubtedly still hold good for us today in our final hour. Speaking about the First Saturday Communion of Reparation, Lucy wrote:

"Whether the world has war or peace depends on the practice of this

---

162   Cited in Frère Michel de la Sainte Trinité, *The Whole Truth About Fatima*, Volume III, Immaculate Heart Publications, Buffalo, New York, pp. 506, 508 (emphasis added).

163   *Cf.* Frère Michel de la Sainte Trinité, *The Whole Truth About Fatima,* Volume II, Immaculate Heart Publications, Buffalo, New York, 1989, p. 820.

164   Pope Pius XII, encyclical *Ingruentium Malorum*, "On Reciting the Rosary," 1951, §15; http://www.vatican.va/holy_father/pius_xii/encyclicals/documents/hf_p-xii_enc_15091951_ingruentium-malorum_en.html

devotion, along with the Consecration [of Russia] to the Immaculate Heart of Mary. …

"Our Lady promised to delay the scourge of war if this devotion was propagated and practiced. We see that She will obtain remission of this chastisement to the extent that efforts are made to propagate this devotion.…"[165]

Father Gruner also gives us a perspective on our essential role, as ordinary laymen or simple priests, in bringing about the Consecration of Russia through these reparatory devotions to the Immaculate Heart:

"When Moses led the Israelites out of Egypt, the Egyptians (who had at first agreed to give them their freedom) changed their minds, and came after them to destroy them. The Israelites were trapped between the Red Sea and the Egyptian army, whose swords were drawn, ready to kill them all. Then God put the physical salvation of that whole people into the hands of one man, Moses. And he told Moses to hold his rod over the Red Sea, and by Moses' obedience to God's command, they were all led through the Red Sea — by none other than the Virgin Mary (that is, the virgin Miriam, the sister of Moses, who symbolized the Blessed Virgin's role in our salvation). So all the people of God were saved through the obedience of the one God-sent leader.

"That real and dramatic event of Old Testament times symbolizes the Catholic Church and the Catholic faithful today. Most of us do not recognize that we are surrounded by enemies who have their swords drawn, ready to kill the Catholic faithful, physically. Nor do most people realize that they can only be delivered, ultimately, by the obedience of the Pope to the command given to him by God, to consecrate Russia to the Immaculate Heart of Mary.

"We are surrounded and we are being crushed little by little, yet most of us don't see it. And the only solution is to obey Our Lady of Fatima in the precise manner that God has dictated, regarding the Consecration of Russia and the devotion of the First Saturdays.

"We might say, 'I can't do much. I'm not the Pope. I'm not a bishop.' Nevertheless, there is much that God and Our Lady are asking us to do. The salvation of a great number of souls depends on us. As Pope Pius XII pointed out,[166] it's a great mystery but the number of souls saved depends

---

[165] Letters of March 19 and June 20, 1939 to Father Aparicio, cited in Frère Michel de la Sainte Trinité, *The Whole Truth About Fatima,* Volume II, Immaculate Heart Publications, Buffalo, New York, 1989, p. 273.

[166] Pope Pius XII, Encyclical *Mystici Corporis,* "On the Mystical Body of Christ," 1943, §44: "Dying on the Cross, [Our Savior] left to His Church the immense treasury of the Redemption, towards which she contributed nothing. But when those graces come to be distributed, not only does He share this work of sanctification with His Church, but He wills that in some way it be due to her action. This is a deep

on how well Catholics cooperate with God's grace.

"Our Lady of Fatima put it in another, much more personal way, when She said, 'Many souls go to hell because they have no one to pray for them and to make sacrifices for them.'

"Now if She wanted to, the Blessed Virgin could appear to the Pope and to the Cardinals in order to move them to perform the Consecration, but She has chosen Her own methods for bringing about Her victory. Each of us has been chosen by God in some way to let the Blessed Virgin work through us to bring about Her triumph. I have come to realize more and more that it really is in the hands of the priests and laity, more than of the bishops and of the Pope, at least at this stage of Our Lady's triumph.

"And so even though we don't see the result of our daily prayers, or of encouraging our parishioners and people that listen to us to pray the Rosary every day, the fact is that this is primarily a spiritual battle. And this battle will be won by the forces of grace, *when we use the means of grace.*

"We all need to pray for the Pope and the bishops to consecrate Russia. This is not about being against the Pope or against the bishops. Ultimately, it is in their hands, and if our generation is going to be delivered, the Pope and the bishops must obey Our Lady of Fatima and consecrate Russia to the Immaculate Heart of Mary. But in the meantime, to obtain those graces we need to have a crusade of Rosaries and First Saturday devotions."[167]

Pictured above is the church of Our Lady of Guadalupe in Rianjo, Spain. In August 1931, Sister Lucy was staying in the house of her Mother Superior's blood sister nearby to this church. (The Church's official approval of the Fatima apparitions had been announced in 1930, and Sister Lucy was exhausted by the international attention suddenly focused on her. She was sent to Rianjo to rest incognito for a few days, where Mother Superior's sister was the only person in the whole city who knew who she was.)

of sanctification with His Church, but He wills that in some way it be due to her action. This is a deep mystery, and an inexhaustible subject of meditation, that the salvation of many depends on the prayers and voluntary penances which the members of the Mystical Body of Jesus Christ offer for this intention, and on the cooperation of pastors of souls and of the faithful, especially of fathers and mothers of families — a cooperation which they must offer to our Divine Savior as though they were His associates."

[167] Father Nicholas Gruner, "Fatima and Our Lady's Immaculate Heart," *Fatima: Only Way to World Peace*

The Costs of Delaying

For the moment, we are still in a position of strength in which we can effectively respond to Heaven's requests. But if, like the Kings of France, we continue to delay the execution of Our Lord's command, we will soon meet a punishment similar to theirs. As Our Lord told Sister Lucy in August 1931 — already two years and two months after Heaven's solemn request for the Consecration of Russia on June 13, 1929:

> "Make it known to My ministers, that given they follow the example of the King of France in delaying the execution of My command, they will likewise follow him into misfortune."[168]

The command which Our Lord refers to is, of course, that the Pope and bishops consecrate Russia to the Immaculate Heart of Mary. (Remember that Our Lady announced that the moment had come in which *God* asked for the Consecration of Russia.) But who were these "Kings of France" whose folly has become a proverb even in Heaven?

In the year 1689, the Feast of the Sacred Heart of Jesus fell on June 17th. On that day, a full century before Catholic France was devastated by its revolution of 1789, Our Lord appeared to Sister Margaret Mary Alacoque at the Visitation Monastery of Paray-le-Monial with a request that she was to transmit to King Louis XIV. Our Lord asked that the king solemnly consecrate France to His Sacred Heart, and even place an emblem of the Sacred Heart on the nation's flag. Our Lord promised in return that He would humble all of the "haughty and proud heads" of the king's enemies.

Our Lord specified to Sister Margaret Mary that He had chosen the Jesuit Order to communicate this message of His great designs to the king. Mother de Saumaise of the Visitation Monastery made this revelation known to the Jesuits, and Father de la Chaise was designated by his Jesuit superior to pass it on to King Louis. But as the great Fatima historian Frère Michel of the Holy Trinity tells us, Father de la Chaise refused to pass on the message of the Sacred Heart to the king. (King Louis, however, eventually found out about Our Lord's desires through means other than the Jesuits.)[169]

Like Sister Lucy in our time, Sister Margaret Mary was known to be a chosen messenger of Heaven, as the visionary of the great revelations and promises of the Sacred Heart given in 1673. But in spite of the clear authenticity of Our Lord's message, King Louis decided not to obey. He was the "Sun King," King Louis the Great, the leading power in all of Europe. He did not need Our Lord's help in humbling his enemies — or so he thought. Frère Michel describes how all the glory and power of the French monarchy fizzled away in the great Sun King's own lifetime:

> "[T]he year 1689 marked the turning point of his reign. In spite of all

---

Conference speech, August 20, 2007; http://www.fatimapeaceconferences.com/brazil_2007/transcripts/fatima&olimh.pdf

[168] Frère Michel de la Sainte Trinité, *The Whole Truth About Fatima*, Volume II, Immaculate Heart Publications, Buffalo, New York, 1989, p. 543-544.

[169] Frère Michel de la Sainte Trinité, *The Whole Truth About Fatima*, Volume II, Immaculate Heart Publications, Buffalo, New York, 1989, p. 549.

his ingenuity, and the incessant labors of his virtuous old age, in spite of his heroic patience in the face of the worst reversals, he did not succeed in decisively crushing 'the haughty and proud heads' of his enemies. These 'enemies' were the enemies of France, as well as the most perfidious adversaries of the Roman Church: Calvinist Holland remained unvanquished; the England of William the Orange, which later came under the Masonic Hanoverian dynasty, jealous of the glory and preponderance of France; and finally Protestant Prussia, this aggressor nation which continued to rise after 1701, for the misfortune of Europe.

"The great king died piously in 1701, but isolated and already powerless to prevent the coming catastrophes. His kingdom, deprived of the increase of extraordinary graces and miraculous help of the Sacred Heart, was gravely menaced from without, and undermined from within by the frivolousness, deadly errors, cowardice, and betrayals which soon brought about its ruin."[170]

Louis XIV was succeeded by his five-year-old great-grandson, Louis XV, who likewise paid no regard to Our Lord's request. His successor, Louis XVI, also made no effort to obey until it was too late. On June 17, 1789 — one hundred years to the day after Our Lord had given His command for the consecration of France through Saint Margaret Mary — the lower parliamentary house or "Third Estate" rose up in defiance of the king, declaring itself to be the National Assembly, and claiming for itself the legislative authority in France, to the exclusion even of the king.

Less than four weeks later, the Bastille was stormed and King Louis XVI was imprisoned. Less than four years after that, in January 1793, the king was guillotined — publicly executed, as if he were a criminal for being a Catholic and a monarch. By the following September, the year-long Reign of Terror was underway, and the Revolution has continued to gain ascendancy over Western society ever since.

So Our Lord's words to Sister Lucia are perfectly clear. To continue our delay in obeying Heaven's command for the Consecration of Russia will be our ruin. Our Lord does not allow the graces that He offers to us to be despised indefinitely.

Saint Alphonsus tells us that with God everything is measured, as we read in the Book of Wisdom: "Thou hast ordered all things in measure, and number, and weight."[171] All of the times and graces of our lives are perfectly measured out in God's Providence. After a certain time, graces that have been repeatedly despised are withdrawn.

In the Third Secret Vision, the children saw a series of executions analogous to what King Louis XVI suffered:

"Bishops, Priests, men and women Religious [were] going up a steep mountain, at the top of which there was a big Cross of rough-hewn

---

170   Frère Michel de la Sainte Trinité, *The Whole Truth About Fatima*, Volume II, Immaculate Heart Publications, Buffalo, New York, 1989, p. 550.

171   Wisdom 11:21.

While praying in the chapel at Rianjo, Spain, Sister Lucy received this terrible warning from Our Lord: "Make it known to My ministers, that given they follow the example of the King of France in delaying the execution of My command, they will likewise follow him into misfortune." Thus Our Lord compared the Church's neglect toward His command through Our Lady of Fatima for the Consecration of Russia, to the indifference shown to Him by the Kings of France who for fully 100 years (from June 17, 1689 to June 17, 1789) had refused His command for the consecration of France to His Sacred Heart. If we refuse the means by which Our Lord has offered to deliver us from the wars and persecutions otherwise certain to come, how can we expect to be preserved from the evils ahead?

trunks as of a cork-tree with the bark; before reaching there the Holy Father passed through a big city half in ruins and half trembling with halting step, afflicted with pain and sorrow, he prayed for the souls of the corpses he met on his way; having reached the top of the mountain, on his knees at the foot of the big Cross he was killed by a group of soldiers who fired bullets and arrows at him, and in the same way there died one after another the other Bishops, Priests, men and women Religious, and various lay people of different ranks and positions."[172]

It is this very execution scene that Our Lord is telling Sister Lucy to "make known to His ministers," as a prophecy of their coming terrible "misfortune" for not obeying His command.

Our Lord's August 1931 warning to His ministers is part of the Message of Fatima. When the Vatican Congregation for the Doctrine of the Faith published the Third Secret Vision in June 2000, they also published a lengthy commentary on the Vision. But nowhere in that scandalous commentary did they explain that this day of slaughter depicted in the Vision is the consequence of ignoring Our Lord's command for the Consecration of Russia.

It is a lesson for us all, but especially for those in positions of authority, both in the Church and in secular governments. The terrible punishments which are about to overtake the world will fall in their greatest rigor on religious and important political leaders (both of whom are ministers appointed to serve Our Lord) who, for whatever reason, did not do what they could have done to bring about the fulfillment of Our Lady of Fatima's requests.

The same fate suffered by the King of France awaits the Pope, many bishops and priests, as well as many lay persons who exercise legitimate civil authority in society (since that authority comes to them from God, and thus they are ministers of God as well) if they do not do their part in time.

Our time is now very short, and we dare not continue our delay in obeying Heaven's command for the Consecration of Russia, lest our generation's folly becomes a proverb to future ages. Father Gruner writes:

"This generation has been chosen to be either blessed or cursed by Fatima. We have no other choice. We didn't choose to be born in this generation, but we are here and the choice is ours.

"We may think we have other choices, but we only have one choice. We can either obey Our Lady of Fatima, or not.

"We cannot not obey Her on the pretext that we don't really know what She wants. That's simply not true. Nor can we not obey Her on the pretext that we don't have to do so because it is a 'private revelation.' That also is

172   Congregation for the Doctrine of the Faith, *The Message of Fatima*, June 26, 2000; http://www.vatican.va/roman_curia/congregations/cfaith/documents/rc_con_cfaith_doc_20000626_message-fatima_en.html

not true.

"We can either obey Our Lady and obtain the blessings that She promised — or, as our other alternative, we can refuse to obey Her and obtain the Fatima curse.

"We will be cursed, and we have been cursed up to now, for not obeying Her. And the curse will only get worse until the time finally comes when those who survive will say: 'That generation that ignored Our Lady — we will not make their mistake. We will obey, and get the benefit.'"[173]

As Father Gruner points out, this blessing or curse will affect our whole generation. We're all in this together.

In the Third Secret Vision, above, we see the Pope being executed — not just being killed, but being executed by soldiers — presumably uniformed soldiers, possibly forming a firing squad. The Vision also depicts bishops, priests, religious, and laymen as well, all suffering the same fate, all falling in turn under the hail of those bullets and arrows.

The same fate that befell King Louis XVI awaits the faithful today, and for the same reason.

Let's not let it happen. Let us tell others about the full Fatima Message; let us urge others to do their part. Let us urge our Pope, Cardinals, bishops, and priests to do their part. Let us realize and make others realize that our time is very short.

---

173   Father Nicholas Gruner, original contribution, not previously published.

APPENDIX I

Day of Infamy — Deception at Pearl Harbor

Was the Japanese attack on Pearl Harbor facilitated and enabled by Washington in order to propel the United States into World War II? Some historians are convinced that President Franklin Roosevelt purposely sought out just such an event to overcome America's popular resolve to stay out of Europe's and Asia's wars.

Not all historians accept this explanation of a high-level conspiracy to bring America into the war in Europe by inciting a Japanese attack, but certainly much has been forcefully demonstrated in support of it, beginning with George Morgenstern's 1947 book, *Pearl Harbor: The Story of the Secret War*.[174]

The case is presented that, having solemnly and repeatedly pledged to the American people that he would not send their sons into a foreign war unless the U.S. were attacked,[175] President Roosevelt promptly set about orchestrating that needed attack. Often cited in this regard is Roosevelt's statement to Secretary of War Henry L. Stimson that the great difficulty was "how we should maneuver to force the Japanese to fire the first shot, while not exposing ourselves to too great

President Franklin D. Roosevelt signs the Declaration of War against Japan on December 8, 1941, scarcely 24 hours after the attack on Pearl Harbor. December 7th, he predicted, was a date that would henceforth "live in infamy," but a number of historians wonder if the larger portion of infamy belongs to Roosevelt himself for resorting to provocations against Japan and deceptions in the homeland to overcome popular feelings against America's involvement in World War II.

---

[174] Published by Devin-Adair Co., New York (online text at http://mises.org/document/6679/Pearl-Harbor-The-Story-of-the-Secret-War). On this subject, see also Charles Tansill, *Back Door to War: The Roosevelt Foreign Policy 1933-1941*, Henry Regnery Co., Chicago, Illinois, 1952; Harry Elmer Barnes (Ed.), *Perpetual War for Perpetual Peace*, Caxton Printers, Caldwell, Idaho, 1953 (online text at https://archive.org/details/PerpetualWarForPerpetualPeace1953); John Toland, *Infamy: Pearl Harbor and Its Aftermath*, Doubleday, 1982; and Robert B. Stinnett, *Day of Deceit: The Truth about FDR and Pearl Harbor*, Touchstone, 2001. See also the review of the aforementioned John Toland book by Percy L. Greaves, Jr. (chief of the minority research staff of the 1945-46 Congressional investigation of the Pearl Harbor attack) at http://www.ihr.org/jhr/v03/v03p319_Greaves.html Also of interest are a number of essays published by the Institute for Historical Review, including seven essays by Percy Greaves in the special Winter 1983-84 "Pearl Harbor" issue (http://www.ihr.org/jhr/v04/v04index.html); "Pearl Harbor: Fifty Years of Controversy" by Charles Lutton in the Winter 1991-92 issue (http://www.ihr.org/jhr/v11/v11p431_Lutton.html); and "Pearl Harbor Attack No Surprise" by Roger Stolley in the Spring 1992 issue (http://www.ihr.org/jhr/v12/v12p119_Stolley.html).

[175] Listen to the audio recording of his promise given at the 1940 Democratic Convention at http://whatreallyhappened.com/WRHARTICLES/pearl/www.geocities.com/Pentagon/6315/FDR_1940_Democratic_Convention.wav

a danger."[176]

According to these historians, the "maneuvers" which the President seems to have settled upon for provoking Japan (and for facilitating a successful attack on Pearl Harbor sufficient to outrage the American public) began with the crippling economic sanctions enacted against Japan beginning in 1940 (truly deadly measures, and acts of war). It is also well known that critical pieces of intelligence gathered from decoded Japanese radio interceptions indicating an imminent attack on Pearl Harbor were not passed on from Washington to the naval command in Hawaii.

John Weir of the Institute for Historical Review describes the increasingly severe economic pressure applied against Japan by Roosevelt, including freezing Japanese assets in the U.S. and embargoing desperately needed oil:

> "In September 1940 Roosevelt imposed an embargo on all US exports of scrap iron and steel to the country. On July 26, 1941, he ordered a freeze on all Japanese assets in the United States, which ended trade between the two countries. This was a severe blow to Japan, which depended heavily on the US for its scrap steel, and oil and petroleum products. Roosevelt's order, which amounted to an *economic declaration of war*, threatened Japan's survival as a developed, industrialized nation."[177]

"Threatening Japan's survival as an industrialized nation" seems a euphemistic way of describing Japan's plight under these sanctions. To be more precise, we must realize that economic sanctions can kill people, particularly the poor and the physically weak. (Children are the most vulnerable to deprivations, and are generally among the first to perish.[178] The rich invariably fare better than the poor, since they are able to pay more for the food and medicine which might remain available on a "black market.")

We would do well to use our imaginations for a moment, to try to picture just what it would be like to make the transition from a "first-world" industrialized country back to a "third-world" economy. There would almost certainly be widespread death by starvation and lack of medical care, and perhaps also by the violence of rioting desperate masses seeking food and other necessities. Truly, *sanctions can be as deadly as bullets and are classified by many as acts of war*.

Historian Robert Thompson adds:

---

[176]   Diary entry of November 25, 1941, cited in David Allen Rivera, *A History of the New World Order*, Ch. 6, §3, "The Pearl Harbor Deception"; http://modernhistoryproject.org/mhp?Article=FinalWarning&C=6.3

[177]   John Weir, "Exonerating Pearl Harbor's Scapegoats" (a review of Edward L. Beach, *Scapegoats: A Defense of Kimmel and Short at Pearl Harbor,* Naval Institute Press, Annapolis, 1995), *The Journal of Historical Review*, Nov.-Dec. 1997 (Vol. 16, No. 6), p. 39, emphasis added; http://www.ihr.org/jhr/v16/v16n6p35_Weir.html

[178]   The reader may be surprised to learn that an estimated 500,000 children under the age of 5 died as a result of the U.S.-led economic sanctions placed on Iraq beginning in 1990. This financial and trade embargo remained in place until the 2003 Iraq War, with little mention of the tragic sufferings of the Iraqi people in the Western media. (*Cf.* UNICEF Report, "Results of the 1999 Iraq Child and Maternal Mortality Surveys; Iraq – Under-five mortality" http://fas.org/news/iraq/1999/08/990812-unicef.htm and http://fas.org/news/iraq/1999/08/irqu5est.pdf)

"Here was no mere deterrence; here was deterrence that amounted to provocation. Was the provocation deliberate? Three times, twice to Lord Halifax and once to British premier Winston Churchill, Franklin Roosevelt intimated that he was trying to force 'an incident' that would bring America more deeply into the fray."[179]

When the Japanese navy bombed Pearl Harbor on December 7, 1941, killing more than 2,400 American servicemen, Admiral Husband E. Kimmel was in command of the U.S. Pacific Fleet, headquartered there in Hawaii. Kimmel's chief intelligence officer, Edwin T. Layton, would later write about that terrible day: "Kimmel stood by the window of his office at the submarine base, his jaw set in stony anguish. As he watched the disaster across the harbor unfold with terrible fury, a spent .50 caliber machine gun bullet crashed through the glass. It brushed the admiral before it clanged to the floor. It cut his white jacket and raised a welt on his chest. 'It would have been merciful had it killed me,' Kimmel murmured to his communications officer."

The American public's demand for an explanation of how the humiliating disaster at Pearl Harbor could have come about led to a speedy indictment of Admiral Husband E. Kimmel, the Commander-in-chief of the U.S. Pacific Fleet. A commission of inquiry appointed by President Roosevelt found Kimmel guilty of dereliction of duty (while all of the major political and military figures in Washington, on the other hand, were exonerated by this same "Roberts Commission," chaired by Supreme Court Justice Owen Roberts.)[180]

Kimmel was relieved of command (and even demoted) ten days after the attack. After those initial hearings, Kimmel's requests for a court martial (in which he would have had an opportunity to clear his name) were consistently denied.

But subsequent investigations have fully established that the dereliction of duty taking place in Washington at that time far exceeded Kimmel's blame in the Pacific fleet's unpreparedness for the Japanese attack.

A Naval Court of Inquiry was convened on July 24, 1944 (in response to an act of Congress of July 13) which completely exonerated Admiral Kimmel, blaming instead Admiral Harold Stark (the chief of naval operations at the time of Pearl Harbor) for failing to advise Kimmel of known intelligence prior to the attack.

Then an exhaustive Joint Congressional Committee Investigation into the Pearl Harbor disaster was convened on November 15, 1945, for which the Truman administration released all of

---

[179]   Robert Smith Thompson, *A Time For War: Franklin D. Roosevelt and the Path to Pearl Harbor*, Prentice Hall, New York, 1991, p. 401.

[180]   *Cf.* "Pearl Harbor Review – The Investigations," National Security Agency, https://www.nsa.gov/about/ cryptologic_heritage/center_crypt_history/pearl_harbor_review/investigations.shtml

the relevant classified documents, including all intercepted Japanese radio messages. The committee examined all of the participants in the affair who were still alive, with the exception of the gravely ill Secretary of War Stimson. The findings of this investigation blamed Admiral Kimmel for errors in judgment, but included a censure of President Roosevelt as well, and an indictment against Washington leaders (naming Secretaries Stimson and Knox, Generals Marshall and Gerow, and Admiral Stark) for failing to provide full intelligence to the officers in Pearl Harbor.[181]

More powerful than these official exonerations, however, in changing public opinion about this sad piece of history, has been the testimony of General Albert Coady Wedemeyer, the highly decorated and universally respected veteran Army commander of the Asian theater during World War II. Publishing in 1958, General Wedemeyer begins and ends the lengthy volume of his memoirs[182] with an emphatic avowal that both the attack on Pearl Harbor and the United States' involvement in World War II could and should have been prevented.

"These [intercepted and decoded] messages had finally indicated the time, the place, and the character of the Pearl Harbor attack, days in advance of December 7. ... On December 4th, 1941, we received definite information from two independent sources that Japan would attack the United States and Britain, but would maintain peace with Russia. On December 6, our intercepts told us, the Japanese would strike somewhere the very next day. President Roosevelt had ample time to broadcast a warning that might have caused the Japanese to call off the attack. In any event, we would not have permitted 3,500 Americans to die in Hawaii without an opportunity to fight back. ...

General Albert Coady Wedemeyer (†1989) was a lieutenant colonel at the outbreak of World War II, assigned to the war-plans division of the U.S. War Department, where he was instrumental in planning the Normandy Invasion. In his memoirs, General Wedemeyer attributes the United States' entry into the Second World War through the disaster at Pearl Harbor to the scheming of President Roosevelt, who was determined to honor his secret commitments to Britain in spite of his contrary promises to the American people. (See references below.)

---

[181]   Cf. "Pearl Harbor Review – The Investigations," National Security Agency, https://www.nsa.gov/about/cryptologic_heritage/center_crypt_history/pearl_harbor_review/investigations.shtml

[182]   Gen. Albert C. Wedemeyer, *Wedemeyer Reports!*, Henry Holt Co., 1958.

"The Soviet colossus would not now bestride half the world had the United States kept out of war — at least until Soviet Russia and Nazi Germany had exhausted each other. But Franklin D. Roosevelt, the proclaimed champion of democracy, was as successful as any dictator could have been in keeping Congress and the public in ignorance of his secret commitments to Britain. Commitments which flouted the will and the wishes of the voters who had reelected him only after he had assured them that he would keep us out of the war. The fact that Japan's attack had been deliberately provoked was obscured by the disaster at Pearl Harbor. President Roosevelt had maneuvered us into the war by his patently un-neutral actions against Germany and the final ultimatum against Japan."[183]

Other servicemen have also come forward to straighten the record on Kimmel's behalf. Notable among them is Rear Admiral Edwin T. Layton (who served as Kimmel's chief intelligence officer at the time of the attack) and Captain Edward L. Beach (who gained international fame in 1960 as commander of the first submarine to circumnavigate the world without surfacing, retracing the route taken by Magellan in 1519).

Each of these authors maintain[184] that Kimmel had been made a scapegoat for a disaster caused by an assortment of Washington higher-ups who prevented Kimmel and his staff from receiving critical intelligence findings (such as the decoded messages being sent from Honolulu to Tokyo by a Japanese spy, Takeo Yoshikawa, who was observing and reporting daily on the exact positions of ships in Pearl Harbor using a grid system that was obviously designed for targeting torpedoes and bombs).

In a 1958 interview, Kimmel named President Roosevelt as the one who bore the responsibility for the nation's greatest military disaster:

"My belief is that General Short and I were not given the information available in Washington and were not informed of the impending attack because it was feared that action in Hawaii might deter the Japanese from making the attack. Our president had repeatedly assured the American people that the United States would not enter the war unless we were attacked. The Japanese attack on the fleet would put the United States in the war with the full support of the American public."[185]

A dark picture emerges. As Dean Manion of the Institute for Historical Review writes,

"The American people did not know then that the president and his top

---

[183]   Cited in Dean Clarence Manion, "An Interview with Admiral Kimmel," *The Journal of Historical Review*, Vol. 11, No. 4, Winter 1991, pp. 495, 497; http://www.ihr.org/jhr/v11/v11p495_Manion.html

[184]   *Cf.* Edwin T. Layton, Roger Pineau, and John Costello, *And I Was There: Pearl Harbor and Midway – Breaking the Secrets*, William Morrow, New York, 1985, and Edward L. Beach, *Scapegoats: A Defense of Kimmel and Short at Pearl Harbor,* Naval Institute Press, Annapolis, 1995.

[185]   Dean Clarence Manion, "An Interview with Admiral Kimmel," *The Journal of Historical Review*, Vol. 11, No. 4, Winter 1991, pp. 495, 497; http://www.ihr.org/jhr/v11/v11p495_Manion.html

military advisors in Washington had been intercepting Japanese secret messages for many months, and that … this dreadful and important information had been deliberately withheld from the men who were most entitled to know it, namely, the top commanders of the United States Army and Navy forces in Hawaii. …

"A few days after the bombs fell [at Pearl Harbor], President Roosevelt made a radio speech to the American people in which he condemned the treachery that propelled us into war, and called Sunday, December 7, 1941 a day that will live in infamy. Mr. Roosevelt was never more truly prophetic than he was when he spoke those words. The infamy of Sunday, December 7, 1941 becomes increasingly notorious with each passing year. Ever more and more certainly that calamitous day is being firmly established in history as the infamous time when more than 3,000 American soldiers and sailors were sentenced to sudden and violent death by the calculated and deliberate dereliction of their own Commander-in-Chief."[186]

As mentioned above, a number of historians are reluctant to subscribe to this highly compelling explanation of FDR's maneuvering of America into the war. One cannot help wondering if this reluctance stems in many cases from a fear of endangering their professional tenures, which rely on "thought-controlled" government grants. In any case, it seems quite telling that official information sources regarding the Pearl Harbor controversy remain unavailable to the public even today, almost 75 years after the events in question, while documents and recordings related to issues such as the Tonkin Gulf incident and Operation Northwoods (occurring decades after the Pearl Harbor attack) have already been fully declassified.

Those historians who insist on disparaging the contention that the Japanese attack at Pearl Harbor was provoked and maximized for propaganda purposes by President Roosevelt (and his willing accomplices within the government) may someday have to concede to the facts, if the still-sealed files of the U.S. government are ever finally disclosed. The ongoing concealment of official documents regarding Pearl Harbor to this day is a strong testimony to the already very compelling evidence that the Japanese attack was intentionally provoked by FDR to get the U.S. into World War II.

In this regard, Father Gruner asks:

"How long will it take for humanity to wake up to this tactic of being sucked into wars it doesn't want? The answer is that only Our Lady of Fatima can stop this madness. It is time we at least try Her solution instead of following blind leaders who lead us to fall into the pit with them."

---

[186] Dean Clarence Manion, "An Interview with Admiral Kimmel," *The Journal of Historical Review*, Vol. 11, No. 4, Winter 1991, p. 496; http://www.ihr.org/jhr/v11/v11p495_Manion.html

APPENDIX II

Deception at Gulf of Tonkin

Here is what Charles Goyette wrote about the Gulf of Tonkin Incident — which became the pretext for the Vietnam War — in his book, *Red and Blue and Broke All Over:*

"Truth is often said to be the first casualty of war. The deceit often begins even before the soldiers march and the bullets fly. On August 5, 1964, a *Washington Post* headline read '*American Planes Hit North Vietnam After 2nd Attack on Our Destroyers; Move Taken to Halt New Aggression.*'

"The Gulf of Tonkin incident the story described consisted of two events. On August 2, as part of a program called Operation Plan (OPLAN) 34A, U.S. Special Forces assisted South Vietnamese forces in an attack on a North Vietnamese radio facility on an island off its coast. The USS Maddox was maneuvering in sync with those attacks, part of an ongoing 'off the books' campaign of military pressure on the north.

"The Maddox was engaged in a fight by three North Vietnamese PT boats. It took four years for Defense Secretary Robert Strange McNamara to admit to Congress that U.S. ships had been participating in South Vietnamese attacks on the north.

"Under the circumstances, the August 2 incident went unnoted. It took a second event, on August 4, for President Johnson to seize the opportunity for war.

"Wasting no time, with a presidential election just three months away, Johnson went on national television that same day describing to the American people 'a number of hostile vessels attacking two US destroyers with torpedoes.' Johnson immediately authorized air strikes on North Vietnam.

"Two days later, Congress passed the Gulf of Tonkin Resolution, giving Johnson the same sort of broad authority to use conventional military forces in Southeast Asia that George W. Bush would later be given for war in the Mideast.

"Here's the way *Time* magazine reported the August 4 North Vietnamese attack:

"*Through the darkness, from the West and South, the intruders boldly sped. There were at least six of them, Russian-designed Swatow gunboats armed with 37-mm and 28-mm guns, and P-4's. At 9:52 they opened fire on the destroyers with automatic weapons, and this time from as close as 2,000 yards. The night glowed eerily with the nightmarish glare of air dropped flares and boat's searchlights. Two of the enemy boats went down.*

"It's a harrowing account, and precise right down to the caliber of the guns and the moment of attack. A fine piece of journalism except that, like the tales of weapons of mass destruction that didn't exist in Iraq, it wasn't true. The second attack on the Maddox didn't happen.

"Well before Johnson addressed the nation, long before he authorized a retaliatory airstrike, the commander of the task force in the Gulf of Tonkin, Captain John Herrick, was advising that the whole event was 'doubtful.' He quickly cabled his doubts to his superiors: 'Freak weather effects on radar,' 'overeager sonarmen,' 'No actual visual sightings,' 'Suggest complete evaluation before any further action taken.' 'Entire action leaves many doubts ...'

"James Stockdale was a prisoner of war in North Vietnam and after he was freed rose to the rank of navy admiral. But on August 4, 1964, he was a squadron commander in the Gulf of Tonkin flying overhead during the attack that didn't happen. Stockdale was ordered to keep quiet about the ghost attack, but after seven years as a POW, he thought the truth mattered enough to be told.

"'[I] had the best seat in the house to watch that event, and our destroyers were just shooting at phantom targets—there were no PT boats there. ... There was nothing there but black water and American fire power.'

"A year after the non-event, President Johnson told his press secretary, Bill Moyers, 'For all I know, our Navy was shooting at whales out there.'

"A National Security Agency report on the Tonkin Gulf incident that was declassified in 2005 was explicit: 'No attack happened that night.' The report could have been released two years earlier, according to the *New York Times*, but officials were afraid it would undermine plans for Bush's invasion of Iraq."[187]

---

[187]   Charles Goyette, *Red and Blue and Broke All Over*, Sentinel HC, 2012.

The victims murdered aboard Malaysia Airlines Flight 17 (MH-17) in eastern Ukraine on July 17, 2014 may have endured a terrifying plummet to the ground similar to that experienced by those aboard Pacific Southwest Airlines Flight 182 in September 1978 (pictured above). The great difference between the two disasters was that MH-17's demise was no accident. It was deliberately shot down. On whose soil will the next war-triggering event be carried out?